Coptic Saints and Pilgrimages

Coptic Saints
and Pilgrimages

Otto F.A. Meinardus

The American University in Cairo Press
Cairo New York

Dar el Kutub No. 13904/07
ISBN 978 977 416 126 1

Dar el Kutub Cataloging-in-Publication Data

Meinardus, Otto F.A.
Coptic Saints and Pilgrimages / Otto F.A. Meinardus.—Cairo:
The American University in Cairo Press, 2007
p. cm.
ISBN 977 416 126 2
1. Saints I. Title
273.52

1 2 3 4 5 6 7 8 9 10   12 11 10 09 08 07

Printed in Egypt

Contents

Preface

COPTIC *Saints and Pilgrimages* should be seen as a complementary volume to *Two Thousand Years of Coptic Christianity*, which deals with the often neglected and disregarded folk religion of the Copts.

Ever since the days of Pope Cyril VI (1959–71), Coptic church leaders have been engaged in wide-ranging ecumenical debates about theological questions of the so-called official religion, including aspects of the christology and ecclesiology of the churches. In view of our 'shrinking world,' this dialogue was and still is vitally important. Age-old theological obstacles that had separated Western and Oriental Orthodox churches have been largely overcome through the unbiased mutual recognition of the respective theological positions. Scholars have recognized that many debates of the past had their roots in strictly nonreligious factors, such as political and economic endeavors, as well as in the idiosyncrasies of non-biblical, Hellenistic linguistic terminology.

For the large majority of Coptic believers, christological concepts like *ousia* and *hypostasis* and the fine differences between *monos* and *mia* were utterly meaningless. The names of places of theological conferences—whether in Århus (1964), Bristol (1967), Geneva (1970), Addis·Ababa (1971), or Chambésy (1985, 1990)—had no relevance whatsoever in the religious lives of the Christians of the Nile.

It is the purpose of this book to call attention to the fact that in addition to the official cult, with its emphasis on Orthodox doctrine and liturgy, there has always coexisted a dynamic popular or folk religion. As opposed to the official cult, which by its sacramental nature is exclusive (insofar as only the properly initiated, the baptized, and duly anointed are permitted to participate), the folk religion, or the popular cult, of the Copts is inclusive. It touches every aspect of the personal and social life of all people. This means that the uninitiated, including non-Orthodox Christians as well as Muslims, can participate. While the official cult is strongly influenced by Hellenistic (Alexandrian) modes of thinking and speech, many of the folk religious attitudes and practices have their roots in the religious heritage of pharaonic Egypt. At the same time, however, the two aspects of religious experience overlap considerably. It must be understood that the uneducated and unsophisticated believers are unable to comprehend the theological nuances couched in the abstract thought of ecclesiastical dogmatics. To satisfy their spiritual needs, such untrained believers are dependent on religious patterns and symbols that have their origin in the devotional practices of their pre-Christian ancestors. *Coptic Saints and Pilgrimages* is an attempt to describe this important aspect of Egyptian religious life.

Most of the material presented in this volume has appeared in one form or another in several scholarly publications. Wherever necessary, corrections and additions to the original texts have been made. A list of the sources in which this work originally appeared is provided in the bibliography.

Again, I want to express my gratitude to Zora O'Neill, who has carefully read the manuscript and has made important and relevant corrections and suggestions. Also, I want to thank the staff of the American University in Cairo Press, who have made this publication possible.

Introduction

❧❧❧

Saints

OVER the centuries, the word 'saint' has taken on different meanings. In the New Testament, all believers in Jesus Christ were called saints. Paul applied the term to the whole church without distinction. He did not withhold the title even from the members of the quarreling, disorderly, problem-infested church at Corinth. If a man is a Christian, according to the apostle, he is a saint: "So then you are no longer strangers and sojourners, but you are fellow citizens with the saints and members of the household of God" (Eph. 2:19). The English term 'saint' is a translation of three biblical words, two of them Hebrew and one Greek. The Hebrew *hasidh* means 'one who is filled with love and loyalty to God'; *qadhash* means the 'loyal ones.' The Greek *hoi hagioi* may be translated 'those who belong exclusively to God.' A saint, therefore, is to be counted among the loyal ones who love God and belong exclusively to him. Nowhere in his letters does Paul speak of an isolated, individual saint. He always assumes that they are grouped in churches.

Sainthood is an ambiguous term. On the one hand, in the word's popular nuance, a saint is a person who appears virtuous, righteous, and respectable. On the other hand, sainthood is also a strictly ecclesiastical concept. The biographies in the Coptic *synaxaria* describe the lives of hundreds of saints. They have in common their 'dehumanized' vitae: each is portrayed as a model of sinlessness and innocence, willing to surrender the self to the glory of God, through either martyrdom or endless suffering through painful, self-inflicted ascetic exercises. In this sense, the meaning of sainthood of the Coptic biographers differs radically from the accounts of the lives of the Old and New Testament men and women, who are portrayed with all their faults, weaknesses, and frailties.

The process of canonization is similar in the churches of apostolic origin. Generally, a candidate passes through three stages. In the Coptic Church, the local bishop proposes the name of a person known to have the necessary spiritual and moral qualifications to the members of the pontifical liturgical commission, which examines the facts. Then the case is presented to the Holy Synod, consisting of the metropolitans and bishops of the church under the chairmanship of the pope. Once approved, the saint is assigned a day of veneration in the Coptic calendar of saints, or synaxarion, based on the time of his or her martyrdom or death. Coptic iconography portrays him or her with a nimbus, and the saint receives liturgical veneration as well.

Pilgrimages

The practice of going on a pilgrimage is deeply embedded in the Judeo-Christian tradition. Jews participated in the pilgrimage to offer sacrifices in the temple. According to Deuteronomy 16:16–17, three times a year, all Jewish males were to appear before the Lord God at the temple: during the feast of unleavened bread (Passover), the feast of weeks (Pentecost, or the first fruits of the harvest), and the feast of booths (Tabernacles). From all parts of Galilee, Samaria, Judea, and the diaspora, Jews went to the 'House of the Lord,' as was decreed to give thanks to the name of the Lord (Ps. 122:4), a law that was also followed by Jesus.

From apostolic days, Egyptians visited Jerusalem. Luke records that Egyptians were among those who received the Holy Spirit on the first day of Pentecost in Jerusalem (Acts 2:10). If any of them returned to their country, they may have formed the nucleus of the first Christian community in Egypt. The Christian pilgrimage arose from believers who visited those sites invested with memories of their Lord's ministry, suffering, death, and resurrection. Sanctuaries were erected over these places and endowed with spiritual powers. Relics connected with Christ's suffering and death were imbued with the utmost religious importance. With the discovery of the Holy Cross by Queen Helena in 328 and the subsequent building of the Church of the Resurrection over the tomb of Christ, Jerusalem became the principal site for Christian pilgrimages.

One of the best-known fourth-century pilgrims was Saint Mary of Egypt. An actress and courtesan, she joined a group of pilgrims to the Holy Land. Once there, the Virgin Mary appeared to her, inspiring Saint Mary to spend the last forty-seven years of her life in penance in the desert beyond the Jordan River. Reports of other Egyptian pilgrims to the Holy Land are common in the fifth through eighth centuries. By the beginning of the ninth century, the Copts maintained their own church in Jerusalem, dedicated to Mary Magdalene and located near Herod's Gate.

By the middle of the thirteenth century, a Coptic archbishopric of

Jerusalem was well established to serve Coptic pilgrims to the Holy Land, among them Pope Gabriel III (1268–71). Beginning in the fourteenth century, European pilgrims mentioned the Copts as one of the communities in the Church of the Resurrection. Coptic pilgrimages to the Holy Land continued throughout the Mamluk and Ottoman administrations. With the help of Archbishop Theophilus of Jerusalem (1935–45), a Coptic Orthodox Society for the Promotion of Pilgrimages to Jerusalem was established. Facilities for Egyptian pilgrims in and around Jerusalem were constructed to accommodate the increasing number of Coptic visitors.

Since the signing of the Camp David peace accords between President Anwar Sadat and Prime Minister Menachem Begin in 1979, Pope Shenuda III has reiterated his prohibition of Coptic pilgrimages to the Holy Land as long as the Zionists occupy Arab Jerusalem and tolerate the Ethiopians in the Coptic property of Dair al-Sultan, on the roof of the Church of the Resurrection. To enforce this stand, Pope Shenuda III has excommunicated numerous Copts who have violated his orders.

While pilgrimage sites dotted the Holy Land for many centuries, their counterparts in Egypt emerged around the tombs of the martyrs, who were the local spiritual heroes of the communities in the Delta and the Nile Valley. Pilgrims were convinced that divine succor, as well as a never-ending series of miracles, could be found at these places. In the Western world, pilgrimages became associated with the doctrine of forgiveness of sins and the acquisition of indulgences. For the Copts, by contrast, pilgrimage is a visible demonstration of Christian faith in a non-Christian environment. The pilgrimage is the Coptic expression and desire to be close to Christ, the Holy Virgin Mary, and the saints.

Biblical Saints in Coptic Spirituality

The Holy Virgin Mary

No biblical person has been more used and misused for political intentions, designs, and purposes by secular and ecclesiastical sovereigns than the Holy Virgin Mary. Kings, popes, and patriarchs have repeatedly turned to the Mother of God to materialize their political interests. For several centuries, she served as 'supernatural defender' and 'guardian' of such cities as Constantinople, Kazan, Pskov, Novgorod, and others. For more than a thousand years, she protected the Christians against Islamic threats. As the 'invincible helper,' she participated again and again in the defense of Constantinople, where the most precious of all Christian relics, the veritable Palladium, the Virgin's robe, was kept. Other churches of this city claimed to possess the Virgin's girdle or the miraculous icon of the Mother of God, wrought by the evangelist Luke. All this persisted until Tuesday, March 29, 1453, when the troops of Mehmet II Fatih conquered Constantinople. With the fall of 'the new Jerusalem,' 'the heavenly city on the Bosporus,' the myth of the 'unconquerable protectress' of Orthodoxy faded away.

A century later, however, her influence was revived by the Roman Catholic hierarchs. As an expression of gratitude for the intervention of the Holy Virgin in the sea battle of Lepanto (the Gulf of Corinth) against the Turkish fleet on October 7, 1571, the feast of the Holy Rosary was introduced for all churches with a Holy Rosary altar. In recognition of the victory of the Christian troops under Prince Eugen over the Muslims at Peterwardein in Hungary on August 5, 1716, the feast of the Holy Rosary became binding for all Roman Catholics. In gratitude for the victory of the Christian forces over the Turks at Vienna on September 12, 1683, Pope Innocent XI (1676–1689) instituted the feast of the Name of the Holy Virgin Mary (Nominis Mariae). Another feast of the Virgin Mary (Blessed Virgin Mary de Mercede), pledged by Pope Innocent XII (1691–1700), commemorated the liberation of Christians from Islamic prisons.

Altogether different from the ways in which Greeks, Russians, and Roman Catholics have used the services of the Holy Virgin Mary, the Copts have seen her as mediatrix between Christians and Muslims, especially in the nineteenth and twentieth centuries. In such national crises as the fight against the British (1882–1922) or the Israelis (1948–79), Christians and Muslims have recognized in the Holy Virgin Mary certain theological affinities that enabled them to join in common demonstrations against the political foe. Although the christological content of the Coptic mariology is quite different from the Islamic one, there are sufficient similarities to see in her 'the golden bridge.'

The theology and piety of the Copts show deep Marian characteristics. Mary is the Theotokos ('God-bearer'), the perpetual virgin *(al-'Adhra')*, and the mistress (Sittina Maryam). Although Mustafa is generally an Islamic man's name, Copts refer to Mary as *al-mustafiya,* the elected or chosen one. The *Theotokia,* poetry praising the Virgin Mary, are an essential part of Coptic liturgical life. Coptic mariology sees her as the tent of the congregation, because the cloud, the divine presence, abides there (Ex. 40:35). She is the true ark of the covenant, which remained for three months in the house of Obededom before David brought it into the city (2 Sam. 6), because she remained for the period of three months in the home of Elisabeth (Luke 1:56). Mary is also the pure golden vessel of the hidden manna, which is the bread of life (John 6:49–51), as well as the candlestick of pure gold, which carried the eternal life (Ex. 25:31). Like all orthodox Christians, the Copts see in her the 'burning bush' that was not consumed, a symbol of the Immaculate Virgin. She is also identified with Aaron's rod, which brought forth buds and blossoms and yielded almonds (Num. 17:8), another symbol of virginity, as well as with the ladder of Jacob (Gen. 28:12), the great mountain (Dan. 2:35), Ezekiel's gate (Ezek. 43:1), the swift cloud upon which the Lord rides and comes into Egypt (Isa. 19:1), and the New Jerusalem (Rev. 21:2).

The Coptic Church adheres to some specific data pertaining to the biography of the Virgin Mary. On Misra 7 (August 13), the angel Gabriel appeared to pious Joachim to announce that Anna, his wife, would give birth to a daughter, Mary. The Copts commemorate the Nativity of the Virgin Mary on Bashans 1 (May 9). For her first three years, Mary remained with her parents. Then they dedicated their daughter to serve in the temple of Jerusalem, where she was fed by angels. When Mary was six years old, her father passed away; two years later her mother died. When she reached the age of twelve, the priests declared her marriageable. They called together twelve pious and God-fearing men of the tribe of Judah to appear with their rods in order to select a groom for the Virgin Mary. A dove settled on Joseph's rod, and was interpreted as a divine sign that the venerable old man had been elected the spouse of the Holy Virgin. According to Coptic tradition, Mary was either twelve, fourteen, or fifteen years of age when Joseph took her as his wife.

The Copts maintain that a certain Matthat ben Levi of the family of Aaron and the tribe of Levi had three daughters (commemorated on Amshir 16/February 23). The oldest one was Mary, the mother of Salome, who served as midwife for the birth of Jesus and confirmed Mary's virginity following the birth. The second daughter, Sophia, was the mother of Elisabeth, the mother of John the Baptist. Anna, the youngest, was married to Joachim, and was the mother of Mary and the grandmother of Jesus. The Copts celebrate the Annunciation to the Virgin Mary in her sixth month, on Baramhat 29 (April 7). Coptic homilies and psalmodies refer to her labor pains, which are also mentioned in the Protevangel of James. The Coptic Church, therefore, does not adhere to a painless pregnancy and delivery, as the Roman Catholic and Ethiopic churches do.

Jesus Christ was born on Kiyahk 29 (January 7) in the year 5510 of the Byzantine era. Two years later, the magi of the house of Balaam (Num. 23:28 f.) appeared to Mary and her son. On Bashans 24 (June 1), the holy family escaped from the wrath of Herod and reached Egypt, where they remained for three years, six months, and ten days. On Ba'una 8 (June 15), they visited al-Mahama (Musturud, on the Ismailia Canal north of Cairo), where the Holy Virgin washed her son in the waters of the well.

The Holy Virgin died on Tuba 21 (January 29) at the age of sixty. Twelve years she had spent in the temple, thirty-four years she had lived in the house of Joseph, and fourteen years she had remained a widow until the ascension of her son. According to another Coptic source, the Holy Virgin died at the age of fifty-eight, eight months, and three days. The bodily Assumption of the Holy Virgin occurred on Misra 16 (August 22). The apostles saw her sitting on the right side of God the Father and blessing them.

There is no single typical Coptic icon of the Holy Virgin that has been venerated over the centuries. Each generation has created its own image according to the theology and piety of the age. The most creative artistic period among the Egyptian Christians lasted from the third to the seventh century. Two iconographical types of the Holy Virgin that determined to some extent the mariology in the Byzantine East and the Catholic West originated in the Nile Valley. The Maria lactans, or Galaktotrophousa, echoed the Egyptian goddess Isis suckling her son Horus, the fertility goddess Renenutet giving her breast to Neper, or Hathor feeding the divine pharaoh Sethos I.

Also, the Eleusa, the virgin of maternal compassion who is aware of the destiny of her son, was an Egyptian creation. This is demonstrated in a famous seventh-century ivory that shows the Christ child hugging his divine mother.

At the same time, however, early Coptic iconography was also influenced by local Byzantine art. This is evident in the sixth- and seventh-century frescoes of the Monastery of Saint Apollo in Bawit. There the Mother of God, majestically dressed and enthroned, holds on her knee her divine son, who already resembles a little adult. This image type led to the common representations of the Hodegetria, Mary pointing to the Christ child as the way to salvation, in Byzantine, Greek, and Russian iconography.

It is tragic that Coptic art could not continue its creative influence on Christian iconography. Undoubtedly, the minority status of the Copts within an iconoclastic Islamic environment was not conducive to the creation of an indigenous Christian art. Even the numerous icons of the Holy Virgin dating from the eighteenth and nineteenth centuries are actually the work of foreigners. Together with the Copt Ibrahim al-Nasikh, the Armenian Ohan Karapetian (Yuhanna Karabid) of Jerusalem painted many traditional icons of the Holy Virgin between 1745 and 1783 for churches in Old Cairo. The works of these two iconographers showed distinct traditional Byzantine and Armenian influences, to which they added specific Coptic elements.

The Coptic iconography of the nineteenth century was largely produced by the arabophone Greek painter Eustathius of Jerusalem, also known as Astasi al-Rumi al-Qudsi. He worked for at least thirty-three years, from about 1838 to 1871, for churches in Upper and Lower Egypt, and for the monasteries and the churches of Cairo. He painted numerous icons of the Holy Virgin as Hodegetria, as a corpulent, oriental queen enthroned with the Christ child on her knee. She is always portrayed with a rather round face, narrow eyes, and a crown. All icons of Astasi al-Rumi are personally signed and carry either a Coptic or an Islamic date. Moreover, the name of the donor is always added. The icons of the Holy Virgin and child by Astasi al-Rumi in the old Church of the Virgin in Dair al-Muharraq and in the Church of the Virgin on Gabal al-Tayr are considered by the faithful to be copies of the original icons painted by the evangelist Luke who is believed to have painted 70 or even 72 pictures of the Holy Virgin.

More recently, the neo-Coptic art of Professor Isaac Fanus of the Institute of Coptic Studies in Cairo has created a wide variety of images of the Holy Virgin Mary. This school is much concerned with the typical Egyptian characteristics in Christian iconography. Although this modern Christian art is widely accepted in Coptic monasteries and the diaspora, the more traditional Copts of the Delta and the Nile Valley are somewhat reluctant to accept it.

Two Roman Catholic images of the Holy Virgin, one from the nineteenth century and another from the seventeenth, have determined to a great extent the mariological piety of large numbers of Copts. In 1830, Cathérine Labouré, of the Convent of the Daughters of Charity in Paris, was the first to see a vision of the Holy Virgin without the Christ child, instead offering with her hands the limitless grace of God, an image type that became known as the Immaculata of the Miraculous Medallion. At the time of Labouré's death in 1876, about a billion medals with this picture had been distributed, many of which undoubtedly had reached Egypt. Recently, numerous public apparitions of Mary in Egypt have taken this same form: in Zaytun in 1968, Idfu in August 1982, Ard Baba Dublu, Shubra, in spring 1986, Dair Durunka in 1990, Shantana al-Hagar in August 1997, Minya al-Qamh in March 1999, and Asyut in 2000. In almost all Coptic churches from Alexandria to Aswan, copies of the Immaculata of the Miraculous Medallion decorate altar screens or altar curtains. Devotional prints in all sizes, as well as plastic and stucco statuettes, are offered in church kiosks and book shops.

The second popular image of the Holy Virgin is the Mater Dolorosa. The fact that Coptic Christianity is strongly determined by mariological devotion and piety explains some recent developments. After all, the Holy Virgin has always been considered the omnipresent, omnipotent protector and defender against all kinds of personal ills and social threats and dangers. The Mater Dolorosa, as depicted by the Florentine master Carlo Dolci (1616–86), is well known and very popular in central and southern Europe. Copies of this picture have been widely disseminated throughout the Coptic communities up and down the Nile. In some instances it has even replaced the paintings and devotional prints of the Immaculata of the Miraculous Medallion. Copies of Dolci's *Mater Dolorosa* are in the Coptic Cathedral of Saint Michael in Aswan, a special chapel in the Convent of Saint Theodore the Warrior at Madinat Habu, and the Church of Saint Bishoi at Dair Anba Bishoi in Wadi al-Natrun, to mention just a few places.

In the Church of Saint George in the village of Wadi al-Natrun, consecrated in 1987 by Metropolitan Pachomius of Buhayra, a color print of Dolci's *Mater Dolorosa* began weeping blood on Wednesday, May 17, 1989. This continued for about a fortnight. Traces of the flow of blood are still noticeable on the picture. Yet it must be noted that this particular poster, which measures 85 by 55 centimeters, is not an exact copy of the original, which is in the State Hermitage Museum in Moscow. Instead of the single tear from Mary's eye on the original, the Coptic picture shows a dark streak of dried liquid, which is believed to represent the flow of blood from her eye.

As in the case of other traditions pertaining to miraculous icons, it is idle to employ the criteria of the natural sciences, such as an investigation of the chemistry of the liquid. It is only as we ask ourselves the question of purpose and relate the manifestation to the social and political climate in which the Copts live that we might find a satisfactory answer to the tears of the Holy Virgin.

Joseph, Spouse of the Holy Virgin

It is said that Ummina Irene, the abbess of the Coptic Convent of Saint Mercurius (Abu al-Saifain) in Old Cairo, decides all substantial issues pertaining to her community based on guidance received either in visions or dreams of her patron saint, Saint Mercurius, or the Holy Virgin. Saint Mercurius has allegedly helped with structural and spiritual developments within the convent, as well as the acquisition of ecclesiastical property west of Alexandria. In this context it is not surprising or strange that Saint Joseph, the spouse of the All-holy Virgin, appeared to Ummina Irene giving direction pertaining to the building of a sanctuary in his honor.

This kind of saintly advice and intervention is not new. In the biblical traditions, especially with regard to Egypt, dreamers and visionaries played a significant role. In fact, the Old Testament patriarch Joseph, who was known as a dreamer (Gen. 37:19), served as a kind of typological prefiguration to the New Testament 'dreamer,' the husband of the Holy Virgin Mary.

Whereas there are no Coptic churches or altars dedicated to Saint Joseph, the husband of the Holy Virgin, there has been a cult of Saint Joseph in the West at least since the Middle Ages. The consecration of a Coptic Orthodox Church of Saint Joseph will be a resuscitation of an ancient Christian tradition. True enough, ever since 1907 Roman Catholic Sisters of Saint Joseph of Lyon have worked in Minya. Moreover, Carmelite Sisters of Saint Joseph have served for decades in Cairo and in Abu Tig. At the same time, the convent chapel will be the only Coptic sanctuary in honor of the spouse of the Holy Virgin. According to information received from Ummina Irene, the Holy See in Rome even offered a valuable relic of Joseph to the Convent of Saint Mercurius in Old Cairo.

The most important sources for the data of the life of Joseph are the Gospels of Matthew, Luke, and John. The apocryphal writings add to his story, as these documents tried to respond to and appease the curiosity of the early Christians. Written in Asia Minor sometime after A.D. 150, the apocryphal Protevangel of James is a narrative extending from the conception of the Virgin to the death of Zechariah. The "History of Joseph the Carpenter," the only document that deals exclusively with the life and death of Joseph, was written in Egypt toward the latter part of the fifth century and exists in Bohairic, Sa'idic, Arabic, and Latin. In addition, the Gospel of Thomas (second century) and the Arabic Infancy Gospel (sixth century) have enriched the legendary cycle of the holy spouse. In his *Ecclesiastical History*, the church historian Eusebius Pamphilus (265–339) mentions a certain Simon, one of the sons of Joseph's first marriage, a cousin of Jesus (III, 11). Sources pertaining to the flight of the holy family to Egypt, of particular interest to the Copts, are the *Homily of the Flight of the Holy Family*, by Zechariah, bishop of Sakha (690–725); the *Vision of Theophilus*, a detailed description of the itinerary of the holy family attributed to the Coptic patriarch Theophilus (384–412); the homily of Cyriacus, bishop of al-Bahnasa (Oxyrhynchus) in the late eighth and early ninth centuries; and the visions of the Holy Virgin Mary which are attributed to the patriarch Timothy Aelurus (457–77). Moreover, both Abu al-Makarim (in the thirteenth-century text *The Churches and Monasteries of Egypt*, attributed to Abu Saleh, the Armenian) and the Coptic synaxarion of the 24th of Bashans (June 1) furnish a rather full account of the sites visited by the holy family in Egypt.

The entry of Abib 26 (August 2) of the Coptic synaxarion informs us of some of the personal data of Joseph. He is said to have died at the age of 111. For forty years he was single, and for fifty-two years he was married to his first wife. He died in the sixteenth year after the birth of Jesus.

Luke (3:23–38) stresses Joseph's priestly parentage, while Matthew (1:1–17) emphasizes his royal descent. Luke traces Joseph's fifty-five ancestors to Adam, the father of the human race. Matthew proves that Jesus is the rightful Messiah by showing his descent from Abraham, David, and the kings of Judah. Luke called the father of Joseph Heli; Matthew named him Jacob. By tracing Joseph's ancestry to Adam, Luke stresses the universality of Christ's mission. Matthew, on the other hand, demonstrated the Jewish descent by mentioning the kings of Judah and the governor Zerubbabel.

Eusebius Pamphilus comments on the discrepancy between the two family trees. Both genealogies were correct since they mention heirs of a second marriage. Moreover, since Mosaic law prohibited marriages among different tribes, the Virgin Mary must have originated from the same family as Joseph (*Eccl. Hist.* I, 7).

The Election of Joseph as Spouse of the Virgin Mary
The Coptic tradition of Joseph the Carpenter records the first marriage of Joseph, in which he had four sons, Judas, Josetos, James, and Simon, as well

as two daughters, Lysia and Lydia. Following the death of his first wife, two of his sons assisted their father in the carpenter's shop in Nazareth.

For the election of the spouse of the Holy Virgin, the ancient, popular custom of the twelve rods was used (Num. 17:2f); rods were symbols of prestige that were carried by the heads of families. The Protevangel of James (8:2 f., 9:1–3) records the consultations of the priests when Mary reached the age of twelve. "They declared: 'Behold, Mary serves the temple at the age of twelve. What shall we do in order to avoid that she may pollute the temple?' And the high priest took the amulet with the twelve bells and withdrew into the Holy of Holies. And the angel spoke to him: 'Zechariah, gather the widowers of the nation. Each of them shall carry a rod. To whom the Lord shall give a sign, he shall be the spouse of the virgin.' Thereupon also Joseph threw away his tools and joined the other widowers. As they were gathered together, the high priest collected the rods and entered the Holy of Holies. After his prayers, lo and behold, a dove escaped Joseph's rod and descended upon the carpenter's head. Thereupon the high priest said: 'Joseph, destiny has assigned to you the virgin of the Lord, do take her under your care.' And Joseph replied to her: 'Mary, I have received you from the Lord and I shall take you to my house.'"

Joseph's Doubts and the Trial of Jealousy

At the time Joseph decided to take Mary into his home, he discovered that she was with child, and "resolved to divorce her quietly" (Matt. 1:19). Joseph's mistrust is understandable. In such circumstances, Jewish law had special proceedings, the so-called 'sota oracle.' The woman who was accused of unfaithfulness had to submit to the biblical test of drinking the bitter water (Num. 5:11–31). The Protevangel of James mentions that both Joseph and Mary had to submit to the trial of jealousy (16:1 f.). In case of any suspicion, the woman had to drink this water of the temple mixed with the dust of the floor of the tabernacle. If she was an adulteress her thigh would rot and her belly would swell. In contrast to later traditions, Matthew records that Joseph relied on a revelation he received in a dream, and this made the ritual of the *sota* oracle superfluous.

On the Way to Bethlehem

The reason for the burdensome journey of the pregnant virgin from Nazareth to Bethlehem was that Joseph was descended from David, and since Bethlehem used to be the city of David (Luke 2:4), the couple had to be registered there. As they were about halfway between Bethlehem and Jerusalem, Mary turned to Joseph to ask him to help her off the donkey, since the child was pressing hard and wanted to be delivered. While Joseph took care of her, he wondered where they could find a place to rest and ease her labor (Protevangel of James 17:3).

In 1993, in the course of widening the main road from Jerusalem to Bethlehem, workers discovered the foundations of a fourth- or fifth-century church. This happened to be one of the earliest churches of Christendom, the *ecclesia kathismatis*, the 'ancient seat.' According to tradition, this church commemorated the site where Mary's labor pains began and she decided to rest. The Arabic Infancy Gospel mentions that from this spot the Holy Virgin, suffering much pain, went on foot to Bethlehem. Hicelia, a pious woman, instructed this church to be built. This story of the setting in of the Virgin's labor at this site is a counterpart to the Old Testament story of Rachel's difficult labor here, which led to the birth of Benjamin (Gen. 35:16-18).

Joseph and the Flight of the Holy Family to Egypt

It is noteworthy that the Coptic traditions about the flight of the holy family to Egypt are based exclusively on dreams and visions. In Joseph's second dream, the angel of the Lord ordered him to take the young child and mother and flee into Egypt (Matt. 2:13). Also, the homily of Zechariah reflects the tradition of the stopovers of the holy family in Egypt, which are attributed to the *Vision of Theophilus*. The detailed itinerary of the holy family depended on Coptic traditions of the early Islamic period.

Coptic traditions refer to the contributions of Joseph as spouse of the Holy Virgin in three places in Egypt: in Bayt Isus (Dair al-Garnus), Qusqam (now al-Qusiya, near Dair al-Muharraq), and in Matariya. The homily of Cyriacus, bishop of al-Bahnasa, mentions a certain Abuna Antonius's discovery of precious vessels and documents from the fourth century. Among other things, it is recorded that the priest Thomas had saved the diary of Joseph from destruction by placing it in a locked chest. This diary is said to have contained Joseph's experiences up to the arrival of the holy family in Bayt Isus, where poor shepherds received him hospitably and Jesus wrought many miracles. This was the reason for naming the village the 'House of Jesus.' Unfortunately, these personal records of Joseph have never been found. Today the Church of the Holy Virgin at Dair al-Garnus, eighteen kilometers southwest of al-Maghagha, commemorates the visit and stay of the holy family with an annual pilgrimage.

In the Dair al-Muharraq north of Asyut, there is an ancient church that the Coptic monks believe to be constructed on the site of the house that the carpenter Joseph built for his family. Abu al-Makarim (thirteenth century) even knew that the holy family used the upper story: "In this chamber there is a window which was opened in the wall by the breath of the Lord; it was not opened by the hand, nor by any tool" (fol. 78 b).

Coptic tradition provided special attention to Joseph's rod, which Jesus had broken into pieces. In the stories of the flight of the holy family to Egypt, Joseph carried the rod that caused numerous wonders in the Delta and in the Nile Valley. According to the *Vision of Theophilus*, Jesus had planted these pieces in al-Qusiya (ancient Cusae, now the site of Dair al-Muharraq), where they took root. The Gospel of Pseudo-Matthew and the Arabic Infancy Gospel place this miracle in Matariya, north of Cairo. This tradition is also reflected in the medieval account of the Ethiopic synaxarion.

Joseph's Illness and Death

The detailed story of Joseph's illness and death is recorded only in the thirty-one chapters of the Coptic "History of Joseph the Carpenter." Joseph was 111 years old when he died, but neither his eyes nor his teeth showed any signs of age. Until his last days he remained clear-sighted, keen, and astute. When his body fell sick, an angel came to him and announced, "This year you shall die." After he heard these words, Joseph went to Jerusalem, entered the temple, confessed his sins in front of the altar, and prayed for forgiveness: "When the days of my life are fulfilled, I pray to Thee, Lord, that Thou mayest send Thy Archangel Michael to help and comfort me, until my miserable soul has left my body without sorrow and pain . . . . May the floods of the stream of fire, that purify all souls, not destroy me . . . ."

Following his devotions in Jerusalem, Joseph returned to Nazareth. He abstained from eating and drinking, and no longer took interest in his work. On the twenty-sixth of Abib, Joseph held a long farewell speech that included an elaborate christological confession. Jesus and Mary were present. Jesus wept and replied to the word of Joseph with compassion and reassurance in the hour of his death. Thereupon, Jesus took his place at the head of Joseph, and Mary sat at his feet (xix, 2). (Some commentators have compared the position of Jesus and Mary with regard to Joseph with that of Horus and Isis at the death of Osiris.)

Joseph could not speak, for the hour of death had overtaken him. Yet just before Joseph passed away, Jesus called his sons and daughters to witness the death of their father. After Jesus offered the prayer of death, he kissed Joseph, and the angels carried his soul. The people of Nazareth who had heard of the death of Joseph gathered together. Jesus washed and embalmed Joseph's body and prepared the funeral according to the custom of the Jews, and he was buried next to his father, Jacob.

The Iconography of Joseph

Whereas Western Christian art of the early and late Middle Ages was very concerned with Joseph, there are probably only a few examples of this subject in Egyptian iconography. In fact, I know of only one wall painting, a severely damaged seventh-century depiction of the trial of jealousy in Dair Abu Hinnis at Antinoë.

The traditional Coptic nativity scenes show Joseph as a venerable old man, squatting on the floor, an insignificant marginal figure, brooding and wondering about the event. In the traditional scenes of the adoration of the Magi and the presentation by the shepherds, Joseph is submissive and humble. The various scenes of the flight of the holy family to Egypt show Joseph carrying the luggage on his rod and leading the donkey bearing the Holy Virgin and the Christ child.

The only icon of Joseph with the Christ child adorns the wall of the Church of the Holy Virgin in Harat Zuwayla in Cairo. This icon was painted in 1869 by Eustathius of Jerusalem (Astasi al-Rumi al-Qudsi). This icon was a present by Qummus Yusuf Rizk to the church.

An interesting painting by the eighteenth-century Austrian artist Josef Adam Mölk (1752) in the Museum of Graz, Austria, is entitled "The Death of Saint Joseph." Undoubtedly, this painting was inspired by the Coptic tradition, probably the Latin edition of the "History of Joseph the Carpenter." In the center of this painting is Joseph's deathbed, with Jesus kneeling at the bedside and lifting the soul, a small, half-naked person, to God. Mary kneels on the other side of the bed holding a lily, a sign of her perpetual virginity. The heavenly reception of the soul is accompanied by the archangel Michael. Carpenter's tools, symbols of Joseph's trade, are seen in the lower right-hand corner.

The Relics of Joseph

Whereas in the Western world the early and medieval cult of relics is almost extinct, the Coptic Church is now experiencing a remarkable revival of the veneration of the relics of their religious ancestors. It is only natural, then, that the sisters of the Convent of Saint Mercurius in Old Cairo are interested in the relics of Joseph.

According to tradition, a relic of Joseph was transferred in 430 from Constantinople to Bologna, the center of the medieval cult of Joseph. Around the year 1000, we hear of Mary's wedding ring that she had received from Joseph. This relic reposed in Chiusi in Tuscany until 1486, when it was given to the citizens of Perugia in Umbria, who deposited it in the Gothic cathedral there, which was just being completed. Joseph's belt was venerated in the Cathedral of Châlons-sur-Marne and in the Chapel of the Feuillants (reformed Cistercians) in Paris, and his staff is kept by the Camaldulensian friars in Santa Maria degli Angeli in Florence. Finally, Joseph's trousers, which were used by the Holy Virgin as diapers for the Christ child, were venerated in the Middle Ages by pilgrims in the Cathedral of Aix-la-Chapelle.

The Assumption of Joseph

Already by the end of the fifth century there existed a tradition according to which the apostles advocated the bodily assumption of Joseph. They asked Jesus why Enoch (Gen. 5:24) and Elijah (2 Kings 2:11) were privileged to receive immortality, while the same honor was not given to the 'just' Joseph, the spouse of the Holy Virgin.

About one thousand years later, some French and Spanish theologians took up the issue concerning the bodily assumption of Joseph. Jean Charlier de Gerson (1365–1429), one of the leading theologians at the Council of Constance, argued in favor of the assumption of the saint. Since there were no substantial bodily relics of Joseph that were being venerated in the churches of Europe, there should be no reason to believe that the body of the saint had not been taken into heaven. This view was also later shared by the Spanish Jesuit Francisco Suárez (1548–1617) and the French theologian Saint Francis of Sales (1567–1622).

The Old Testament Patriarchs and Prophets

The Copts have always looked at the Old Testament stories of the patriarchs and prophets in Egypt with much interest—primarily because the Copts saw themselves as descended from Abraham. Although today there is only one Coptic church dedicated to Abraham, in Dalga, west of Dair Mawas on the edge of the cultivated land, in the twelfth century in Cairo a church was dedicated to the patriarchs Abraham, Isaac, and Jacob.

The Copts entertained a special favor for 'Joseph the Truthful' (an epithet used in the Qur'an, in Surat Yusuf, verse 51). They regard him as one of their ancestors through Asenath, the daughter of Potiphera, priest of On (Gen. 41:45). Not only did Joseph rebuild Madinat al-Fayyum, he also dug 'Joseph's river,' the Bahr Yusuf. Moreover, he built the first Nilometer at Memphis to measure the rise of the Nile by cubit. The pharaoh made him prime minister of the land and clothed him with a robe of honor and entrusted him with his signet ring and with the administration. Jacob, son of Isaac, had a special relation to the Fayyum, especially to the site of the Monastery of Naqlun. There, so the tradition goes, Jacob enjoyed the shade and worshiped in the days of Joseph, when he was superintendent of the buildings of the Fayyum and Hagar al-Lahun.

Moses, his brother Aaron, and his sister Miriam are believed to have been born in Askar, south of al-Fustat in the district of Itfih in the province of Giza. Special mention is given to Moses' devotional life, and the places where he prayed are recorded with special care, as in the case of Damuh in the province of Giza, and at the prison where Joseph was held, at Abusir, now in the district of al-Badrashin. In Memphis residents used to show the place where Moses lay in ambush for the Egyptian he killed (Exod. 2:12).

Of the prophets, Jeremiah, Ezekiel, and Daniel are believed to have found refuge in Egypt, perhaps in the train of Nebuchadnezzar, whose invasion of Egypt is not questioned by Copts or Muslims.

Patriarchs and Prophets as Models for Coptic Hermits

In the spiritual community of hermits in Wadi Rayan under the leadership of Abuna Matta al-Maskin (1960–69), the men who joined the group received the names of Old Testament patriarchs and prophets. Upon questioning as to the reason for this practice, he said, "The Old Testament throws its illuminating rays upon the New Testament, and the New Testament can only be understood by a faithful reading of the Old Testament. The names are not given haphazardly, but according to the marks of the person's spirit and the marks of his heart, which are not easily seen by every man. Moreover, the name that is chosen will leave a powerful and lasting impression on the monk. When we determine which name shall be given to a monk, we all assemble and pray, and then we decide." Thus, the monks received the names of such Old Testament personages as Dawud, Musa, Iliya, Ilisha, Ish'aiya, Irmiya, and Nihamiya.

The Holy Apostles

According to the *Vision of Theophilus,* the apostles participated in the ceremony of the consecration of the first church in the world, the Church of the Holy Virgin Mary in Qusqam, the site of the Upper Egyptian Dair al-Muharraq. Following his resurrection, Jesus Christ commanded a luminous cloud to descend to carry all the apostles, the Holy Virgin Mary, Mary Magdalene, Anna, and Salome to this holy house. This happened in the third hour of Hatur 6 (November 15). When the apostles were ready for the consecration of the church, Gabriel and Michael carried the vessels containing the water that Jesus Christ sprinkled on the church. All the apostles were present at the consecration when Jesus said, "The hands that have fashioned you,

O Adam, have consecrated this house, and the hands in which nails have been driven on Golgotha have blessed this house. Amen." Peter was ordered to celebrate the Divine Liturgy in the new church. Jesus commanded the apostles to remember their parents who had passed away and also ordered the souls of their parents who had departed to come and enter the sanctuary. They came in their bodily form, and he baptized them with water that had remained from the consecration of the church. Then they all received the divine elements of the Eucharist. Afterward a large bird flew down from heaven carrying wines and delicacies, and they took from it what they wanted. Then, at sunset, a cloud took the participants and transported them to their house in Jerusalem.

The apostles are commemorated in the Coptic synaxarion as follows:

Peter of Bethsaida (Abib 5/July 12) occupied a special place among the apostles, in addition to the ecclesiastical responsibilities transmitted to him by Jesus Christ (Matt. 16:19). He was crucified head downward, so that the blood ran out of his eyes, nose, and mouth. In the eighth century, the Copts prayed in the Cathedral of Saint Peter on the banks of the Nile in Giza for the annual flood.

Andrew (Kiyahk 4/December 13) was the brother of Peter. Accompanied by his pupil Philemon, he was sent to the land of the Kurds. He also traveled with Bartholomew to convert the *kynokephaloi,* the dog-headed cannibals. In Achaia he was crucified.

John (Bashans 16/May 24) was the son of Zebedee and Salome. For the Copts, John the disciple, the evangelist, the Presbyter, and the Seer of Patmos are all the same man. He preached in Asia Minor and Ephesus.

James (Baramuda 17/April 25) was the brother of John and the elder 'son of thunder.' He preached in Judea and Samaria and was beheaded by Herod Agrippa I in A.D. 44 (Acts 12:2).

James (Amshir 10/February 17), the son of Alphaeus and Mary Cleopas, composed the Divine Liturgy that is still used by the Armenians. He was a vegetarian, never washed, and clothed himself only in linen. He preached in many lands and converted the Jews. He was bishop of Jerusalem when the emperor Claudius demanded his death. He was buried near the temple.

Philip (Hatur 18/November 27) preached in North Africa, where he was crucified and buried in Carthage.

Bartholomew (Tut 1/September 11) preached together with Peter in the oases of the Western Desert, and later among the Berbers, where he met with dog-headed cannibals. Finally he was sewn into a sack filled with sand and drowned in the sea. In the Middle Ages his relics reposed in the Monastery of Saint Shenuda at Suhag.

Simon the Zealot, or Nathanael (Bashans 15/May 23) was born in Cana, Galilee. He preached in the lands of 'the black people' and went to the island of 'Birtana,' where he healed the lepers with the baptism. He was nailed to the cross. In the Middle Ages his relics were taken to the Monastery of Saint Shenuda at Suhag.

Thaddaeus (Abib 2/July 9) preached the gospel, especially in Syria, where many people believed in Christ.

Thomas, known as Didymus (Bashans 26/June 3), was born in Galilee. He preached in India in the service of Lucius, minister of the king. After Lucius' wife died, Thomas brought her back to life, and Lucius believed and was baptized. Thomas also went to Kantoura (Kandahar?). Even after his death he appeared to many people. The relic of his hand reposes at Mailapur, a suburb of Madras. It is said to be incorruptible.

Matthew (Baba 12/October 22) went to the countries farthest from his home, preached in the temple of Apollo, saw the Lord surrounded by 144,000 angels, and caused a table of food to descend from heaven. The governor Festus commanded that Matthew be beheaded. His body was thrown to the birds, but the believers collected the body and buried him.

Matthias (Baramhat 8/March 17) took the place of Judas. He preached to the cannibals, and later Andrew assisted him. He performed numerous miracles that caused people to accept Christ.

Because they were Christ's disciples and messengers, the holy apostles are an integral part of the Copts' faith in Jesus Christ. In all Coptic churches the twelve apostles appear at the top of the altar screen, often as couples, since they were sent two by two (Mark 6:7), with three couples on either side of the Holy Virgin Mary. On some nineteenth-century altar screens, the apostles appear dressed in Coptic liturgical vestments. The twelve monolithic columns in the nave of the Church of Saints Sergius and Bacchus in Old Cairo most likely represent the twelve apostles.

The most typical Coptic iconographical representation of the holy apostles according to Matthew 10:2–3, Mark 3:16–18, and Acts 1:13 is found on the modern altar screen in the Church of Saint Bishoi at the Monastery of Saint Bishoi, by the Coptic iconographer Isaac Fanus. The apostles on this altar screen are similar to the arrangement of the apostles on the famous sixth-century apse of the Monastery of Saint Apollo in Bawit. They are uniformly dressed in tunics and long mantles. In their left hands they hold either a book or a scroll, while their right hands hold a hand cross, or point to the book, or extend the one-finger Coptic blessing. The rigid facial expressions appear not only lifeless but also uniform: their eyes and eyebrows are almost identical. The distinguishing characteristics of each apostle are confined to the hair and the color and length of their beards.

The Heavenly Host and the Twenty-four Elders of the Apocalypse

Within the context of the theology of the Copts, the heavenly host occupies an important place. There are the seven archangels, Michael, Gabriel, Raphael, Suriel, Zedekiel, Serathiel, and Ananiel, who are the seven spirits of God (Rev. 4:5). Furthermore, the Holy Scriptures mention the six-winged seraphim, which filled the temple with smoke (Isa. 6:2–4), and the cherubim, which provide the throne for the Lord (Ps. 99:1). The angels represent the lowest category of the celestial hierarchy. They are also closest to mankind.

The Scriptures offer several answers pertaining to the various functions and responsibilities of angels. In some cases, they appear in the form of a person, conversing extensively with Hagar, the maid of Sarai (Gen. 16:7); in other situations, the angels are invisible, spiritual, bodiless creatures representing a superior rank in God's creation (Col. 1:16). They protect and guard mankind (Ps. 91:11) and they expel all demons (Tob. 8). On the day of the last judgment, they will separate the evil from the righteous (Matt. 13:49). Moreover, they will carry the souls of the destitute to Father Abraham (Luke 16:22). Angels appeared to Joseph (Matt. 1:20), Zechariah (Luke 1:13), Mary (Luke 1:28), and the holy women at the empty tomb (Mark 16:5). As for their numbers, the Bible provides different answers. Jacob dreamed that angels ascended and descended the heavenly ladder (Gen. 28:12). According to the prophecy of Daniel (7:10), millions of angels served the 'Ancient of Days,' and the seer of Patmos (Rev. 5:11) witnessed an equally large number. But Jesus referred to only twelve legions of angels (Matt. 25:53). On Christmas Eve, we hear of the angel of the Lord accompanied by a multitude of the heavenly host (Luke 2:10–13). For the medieval cabalists there were a total of 300,655,722 angels. The thirteenth-century Dominican theologian Saint Albertus Magnus corrected the Jewish figure and estimated 399,930,004 angels, of whom, however, a third had fallen. Compared to these almost astronomical figures, the Coptic numbers appear quite moderate. An early Coptic text, attributed to Bartholomew, mentions only twelve thousand cherubim, twenty thousand seraphim, and another forty-three thousand celestial beings.

The Copts pay special attention to the archangel Michael. On the twelfth day of each month, they ask him for protection and support. He is credited with determining the annual rising of the Nile flood (Misra 12) and even stopping the movements of the sun (Ba'una 12). At least forty churches in Lower and Upper Egypt are dedicated to Michael, and in most other churches, one altar is named after him. On the occasion of the appearance of the Holy Virgin Mary on the roof of the Church of the Holy Virgin in Zaytun in April 1968, there appeared standing behind the Holy Virgin Mary a huge angel with his wings spread out (Baramhat 24). Many Copts believe that this was Michael, the prince of the heavenly host.

Special psali, or songs of praise, are offered to honor Gabriel, the angel of the Annunciation (Dan. 8:16, Luke 1:19–20) on Baramhat 30 (April 8) and Ba'una 26 (July 3). Raphael commands the celestial powers and protects all those who call upon him, while Suriel is known as the heavenly trumpeter, who "will gather his elect from the four winds" (Matt. 24:31) and raise the righteous from the dead (1 Thess. 4:16; 1 Cor. 15:32) and lead them to paradise (Tuba 27).

In the Coptic tradition apparitions of angels and archangels are quite common. It is, therefore, impossible to present a complete listing of all the various celestial manifestations. The following events are recorded in the Coptic synaxarion: Saints Dioscorus and Aesculapius were strengthened in their faith when the archangel appeared to them (Tuba 1). The angel of the Lord touched the tongue of Saint Ezekiel of Armant (Kiyahk 14) and comforted Saint George of Damira (Ba'una 19). An angel called upon Saint Isaac of Tiphre to prepare himself for martyrdom (Bashans 6). Saint John of Sanhut was guided by an angel to the town of Atripe to testify to his faith (Bashans 8). An angel appeared to Saint John of Lycopolis and ordered him to settle in the desert (Hatur 12), and Saint John Kame received word from an angel to establish a monastery (Kiyahk 25). Saint Macarius was led by an angel into the inner desert (Baramuda 27), and Paphnutius of Dandara was admonished by an angel to seek the crown of martyrdom (Baramuda 20). An angel appeared to Saint Pidjimi and told him to become a monk (Kiyahk 11). During the years 1995 and 1996, many Copts from Cairo and Lower Egypt, as well as many Muslims, experienced numerous apparitions of the archangel Michael in the Church of Saint Michael in the village of Kafr Yusuf Samri, a few kilometers south of al-Zaqaziq in the diocese of Anba Yakubus. According to the testimony of Abuna Samuel Zechariah, the parish priest of the Church of Saint Michael, the archangel appeared in various forms, sometimes as a youth dressed in a white *galabiya* (cf. Matt. 28:3), while others saw the angel in an unusually bright light, and others even testify to having seen the angel with his wings in the nave of the sanctuary. Many miracles were recorded, including demon exorcisms, multiplications of oil, and several healings of edema, hypertrophy, hemorrhoids, tumors, and the like.

These manifestations ought to be seen in light of the present situation in Egypt, in which Copts are members of a minority. Wholeheartedly they trust in the words of the prophecy that "at that time shall arise Michael, the great prince who has charge of your people. And there shall be a time of trouble, such as never has been since there was a nation till that time; but at that time your people shall be delivered, every one whose name shall be found written in the book. And many of those who sleep in the dust of the earth shall awake, some to everlasting life, and some to shame and everlasting contempt" (Dan. 12:1–2).

In addition to the 'good angels,' the Copts also know about Abbaton, the merciless and furious angel who punishes the unredeemed. Moreover there exists Sakliatoboth, or Mastema, known among Western Christians as Lucifer or Satan, the Leviathan (Ps. 74:14). It is interesting to note that Coptic iconography has avoided presenting the angels in the form of the Old Testament tetramorphs, that is, with four faces, each having four wings (Ezek. 1:5–26). On the contrary, the forerunners of the Coptic angels seem to have been the Hellenistic angels, such as the 'flying eros' on a square tunica insert.

In addition to the seraphim, cherubim, archangels, angels, thrones, dominions, principalities, and authorities (Col. 1:16), there are the twenty-four elders of the Apocalypse. They are clad in white garments and carry golden bowls full of incense and join in a new song (Rev. 4:4; 5:8–9). Before the heavenly throne they fall down while praising the Lamb of God (Hatur 24). The oldest iconographic representation of the twenty-four elders, although badly damaged, dates from the ninth or tenth century and can be found in the apse of the church of the Monastery of Saint Simeon in Aswan. Another tenth-century fresco adorns the *haikal,* or altar, of the Chapel of Saint Takla Haimanot in the Church of the Holy Virgin al-Muʿallaqa in Old Cairo. Over the centuries, Coptic parish and monastic churches in Lower and Upper Egypt were adorned with imagery of the Apocalypse, including the twenty-four elders. Among the better known apocalyptic cycles are those in the Chapel of Saint Benjamin in the Monastery of Saint Macarius (eleventh century) and in the Chapel of the Twenty-four Elders in the Monastery of Saint Paul the Theban (1710). In most churches, the paintings of the twenty-four elders decorate the walls of the *haikal,* as in the Church of the Holy Virgin in Rawd al-Farag, Shubra, and the Church of Saint George in Giza.

According to Coptic tradition, the twenty-four elders are named after the twenty-four letters of the Greek alphabet: Akhael, Banoel, Ganoel, and so forth. It is really not surprising that images of the Apocalypse are part and parcel of Coptic artistic tradition: on Easter Sunday all twenty-two chapters of the last book of the New Testament are read; moreover, the four bodiless living creatures (*asomati*) and the twenty-four elders are mentioned in the final blessing at the service of the evening raising of incense.

A few years ago, there was a rather interesting addition to the celestial imagery of the Copts. The iconographers of the neo-Coptic school of art of Professor Isaac Fanus have begun to incorporate pre-Christian, pharaonic images and symbols into traditional biblical subjects. Thus, for example, to the well-known Coptic theme of the flight of the holy family from Bethlehem to Upper Egypt they have added Horus, the ancient Egyptian god of the sky and the stars, in the form of a magnificent bird whose wings touch the limits of the earth. He guides the holy family and Salome the midwife along the Nile Valley to Upper Egypt. Special attention is given to the udjat eye, the eye of Horus, which was damaged by Seth but eventually restored by Thoth. The Christian, however, sees in the well-known *udjat* the 'never-sleeping eye' of God with which he leads his people through heights and depths of their daily life (Ps. 121:3–4).

The Martyrs in Coptic Spirituality

THE word 'martyr' literally means witness. As such, the word has a split personality. On the one hand, it is a worldly habitué of the law courts, where witnesses give evidence during trials by judge or jury or affix their signatures to wills and affidavits. In this sense the term is used in the interrogation of Christ by the high priest (Mark 14:63). On the other hand, the term has assumed the meaning of testifying to a religious truth, as used by Jesus Christ in the parable of the lost sheep (Matt. 18:16). Toward the end of the first century, when the conflict between the Roman state and Christianity became unavoidable, many Christians followed the counsel of the Lord when he told them, "but you shall receive power when the Holy Spirit has come upon you; and you shall be my witnesses in Jerusalem and in all Judea and Samaria and to the end of the earth" (Acts 1:8). In the beginning, every Christian was a witness, a person who had personal knowledge of the Christ-event and could talk of it based on his or her firsthand experience. To witness for Christ was a certain way to eternal life. The Christians of Smyrna received the admonition, "Be faithful unto death, and I will give you the crown of life" (Rev. 2:10). The zeal of Saint Ignatius (A.D. 115), who had asked the Roman Church to do nothing to spare him from the martyr's death, was the natural application of this divine promise.

In Egypt the cult of the martyrs occupied an important place in the history of the church. The medieval Coptic synaxaria list 184 commemorations of the martyrs and only sixty-three for the ascetics of the church. Egyptian Christians often sought death by purposely insulting the magistrates, sometimes even by breaking the idols. Their enthusiasm for martyrdom, for the eternal life, often became self-centered. Nonetheless, these men and women endured terrible tortures—even if one subtracts some of the obvious exaggerations from the martyrologies—rather than abandon their faith. Egyptians were inspired by the pious example of Mark, who had witnessed against the polytheistic traditions and against the divinity of the emperor, and was martyred by an enraged pagan mob in Alexandria (A.D. 68).

To many Egyptians the new Christian faith appeared irreligious, immoral, unpatriotic, and disloyal to the state and society. Thus, some of the early emperors, reflecting the *vox populi*, may have had little choice but to follow the policies of the street. While persecutions were unknown and forbidden by his predecessors, Marcus Aurelius (A.D. 161–80), the noble Stoic philosopher, found the policy of persecution inescapable. The first state-sponsored persecution occurred during the reign of the emperor Septimius Severus (193–211), when he decreed that Christian conversions had to be stopped at all costs. Eusebius Pamphilus (early fourth century) mentioned that particularly in Alexandria "the heroic wrestlers (the athletes of God) from Egypt and the Thebaid were escorted thither as to a mighty theater of God, where, by their invincible patience under various tortures and modes of death, they were adorned with crowns from heaven. Among these was Leonides, the father of Origen, who was beheaded" (*Eccl. Hist.* VI, 1). The next massive wave of persecutions occurred during the short reign of Decius (249–51). With these tribulations, which were exceptionally severe in Egypt, began the series of historically well established martyrdoms. The emperor issued an edict demanding that every citizen procure a document from the local magistrate testifying that he had offered sacrifices to the gods. Those who refused to conform with this order were severely tortured and finally beheaded. In 250, Origen was arrested, imprisoned, and mistreated. However, he survived these troubles and sufferings and died in 254 in Tyre.

The persecutions under the emperor Diocletian (284–305) have provided the great majority of the passions of the Egyptian martyrs. Although he saved Alexandria from famine near the end of the third century (Pompey's Pillar commemorates this deed), Diocletian is most remembered for the severe persecutions of the Christians. He had hoped to strengthen the empire by reviving the old religion, and the church, as an independent religious institution, appeared to be a standing menace to his authority. In 302, soldiers who refused to sacrifice to the Roman gods were dismissed, and in 303 churches were destroyed and Christian property was confiscated. Church services were prohibited, and those who protested against the order were put to death. Eusebius described the situation in Egypt, "where thousands, both men and women and children, despising the present life for the sake of our Savior's doctrine, submitted to death in various shapes. Some, after being tortured with scrapings and the rack and the most dreadful floggings and other innumerable agonies, which one might shudder to hear, were finally committed to flames; some plunged and drowned in the sea, others voluntarily offering their own heads to the executioners" (*Eccl. Hist.* VIII, 8). Church historians provide various estimates about the numbers of martyrs, ranging from 144,000 to 800,000.

To this day, the Copts commemorate the brutal persecutions by Diocletian. The Coptic calendar, the 'Era of the Martyrs' (A.M., or *anno martyrii*), commences on August 29, 284, the year in which Diocletian was chosen emperor, although the great persecution in Egypt did not begin until 303. To convert the Coptic year to the corresponding Gregorian calendar, add 283 if the date falls between September and December, or 284 for all other dates.

The term 'new martyrs' is normally employed for the Christians who suffered and died for their faith during the various Islamic dynasties. However, there was no general policy of the Muslim rulers toward the *dhimmiyin*, the protected 'people of the book,' which included the Copts. This is exemplified in the days of the Umayyad governors (640–750). The governor Maslama allowed the Copts to build a church at al-Fustat (Old Cairo), and 'Abd al-'Aziz ibn Marwan even resided in the Coptic monastery in Tammua, although his nephew 'Abd Allah forbade Christians to wear the burnus and demanded that monks wear special badges. In 722 many Coptic churches were sacked, icons destroyed, and the patriarch imprisoned. Into this period falls the martyrdom of Febronia, a virgin of great beauty who was dragged by Arab soldiers out of her Upper Egyptian convent. After being anointed in preparation for death, she displayed her neck and was beheaded, thereby preserving her maidenhood (Abu al-Makarim, fol. 84 b). A series of regulations by the Abbasid caliph al-Mutawakkil (850) forced Christians to set up wooden images of the devil over their doors and wear honey-colored clothes with distinguishing patches as well as girdles, symbols of femininity. Moreover, they were forbidden to ride horses.

In the days of the Fatimid caliph al-Mu'izz (972–75), the Copts experienced favorable treatment, which was continued by his son and successor al-'Aziz (976–96), but this situation was sadly darkened by the caliph al-Hakim, who led one of the most senseless persecutions of the Copts. Between 1007 and 1012, he offered the Christians the choice of becoming Muslims, leaving the country, or wearing a five-pound cross as a badge of their degradation. A general order was issued for the destruction of all Christian churches and monasteries in Egypt and the confiscation of their land and property.

One of the most serious calamities for the Copts occurred during the early years of Mamluk rule in 1320, when many churches and monasteries in Cairo, Alexandria, and Upper Egypt were destroyed, as described in detail by al-Maqrizi. In the Cairo region alone, fifty-four churches were sacked. One of the better-known martyrs during this period was Saint Tegi (also known as Saint Ruwais or Saint Farig, 1334–1404), whose tomb next to the new Cathedral of Saint Mark in 'Abbasiya is venerated annually on October 28. The list of martyrs during the Mamluk dynasties (1250–1517) is long, and only a few of them can be mentioned in this context. In the last few years, relics of Saint Salib, also known as Saint Stauros, have been venerated in numerous Coptic churches. Born in Hor, near Minya, he lived as hermit, and later confessed his faith before the sultan. He was stoned and beheaded. Other martyrs of the Mamluk period include Abuna Sidrak al-Antuni and five other monks, as well as Elias of Durunka, Bulus of Bani Hasan, Ya'qub and Yuhanna of Sunbat, and others.

When considering the Copts who suffered attacks from fanatic Islamic extremists in the late twentieth century, one should differentiate between those Christians who were killed on account of their religious identity and those who suffered martyrdom because of their fearless witness for Jesus Christ. While in some cases this distinction cannot be properly upheld, there are many violent incidents perpetrated by members of the Gama'at al-Islamiya in which mere Coptic identity was sufficient reason for murder. This may have been the case of those sixty Copts killed on December 12, 1972, in al-Khanka, the ten Christians murdered in the summer of 1981 in al-Zawiya al-Hamra (Cairo), or the twenty Copts assassinated in the Upper Egyptian village of al-Kusha on December 31, 1999. Nonetheless, their deaths remain visible testimonies to their adherence to the church.

There are Copts, however, who have been assassinated because of their witness for Christ. This was certainly the case when nine Coptic young people were shot by Islamists during their prayer meeting on February 12, 1997, in the Church of Saint George in Fikriya (Abu Qurqas), or when Abuna Ruwais, pastor of the Church of Saint John the Baptist in Diwaina (Abu Tig), was murdered on November 24, 1988.

It is impossible to list all of the violent actions of the militant Islamists against their countrymen. According to the statistics of the Center for Egyptian Human Rights, there have been 561 incidents of violence against the Copts since 1994. The few cases mentioned are representative of a situation that Copts have experienced since the days of Diocletian, al-Hakim, and other Mamluk sultans. It is hoped that under the spiritual leadership of Pope Shenuda III and the wise government of Egypt's president, Hosni Mubarak, the Copts will be able to find the kind of inner and social security necessary for a harmonious and peaceful social life.

The Ascetics in Coptic Spirituality

⚜︎⚜︎⚜︎

IN view of "the present distress" and because "the appointed time has grown very short" and "the form of this world is passing away," Paul admonished the Corinthian believers to remain as he was—namely, unmarried (1 Cor. 7:26–31). The belief in the immediate Parousia, the second coming of Christ, was certainly a decisive motivating factor for the methodical effort and exercise to discipline both mind and body for the attainment of Christian perfection. Austerities of various kinds, including fasting, vigils, abstinence from certain foods, chastity, silence, macerations, and mutilations, were practiced to overcome the impulse to sin. The imitation of Christ, as understood by the Egyptian ascetics, was the principal reason for accepting privations and pain with joy. These experiences even transfigured pain and made suffering the summit of perfection. Consequently, there developed among the ascetics a competitive rivalry in degrees of asceticism. Those who were regarded as masters of asceticism were known as the *theophorai*, those 'carrying the divine,' or as the *pneumatophorai*, those 'carrying the spirit.'

Not only the length of fasting but also the physical alienation from the sinful world became a determining factor for attaining the goal of perfection. While some of the ascetics withdrew many miles into the inner desert, Saint Agathon (Tut 14/September 24) followed the example of Saint Simeon the Stylite (388–460) and spent fifty years on a pillar near Sakha in the Nile Delta. In the Monastery of the Syrians in Wadi al-Natrun, the monks show the cell where Saint Bishoi used to pray day and night, his hair tied to a hook to prevent him from falling asleep.

In the Gospel of Matthew, Jesus speaks of those "who have made themselves eunuchs for the sake of the kingdom of heaven. He who is able to receive this, let him receive it" (19:12). Moreover, the disciple of Jesus Christ must renounce his family: "If any one comes to me and does not hate his own father and mother and wife and children and brothers and sisters, yes, and even his own life, he cannot be my disciple" (Luke 14:26), and a reward is promised to those who leave house or wife or brothers or parents or children for the sake of the kingdom of God (Luke 18:29-30). Indeed, the New Testament ascetic attitude sees the family as an encumbrance. "The sons of this age marry and are given in marriage; but those who are accounted worthy to attain to that age and to the resurrection from the dead neither marry nor are given in marriage, for they cannot die any more, because they are equal to angels and are sons of God, being sons of the resurrection" (Luke 20:34–36). Moreover, Christ himself remained chaste.

In spite of the fact that marriage was always considered good, and a 'great mystery,' the Coptic Church retained the doctrine of the superiority of virginity to married life. The leadership of the church, including the bishops, metropolitans, and patriarchs, has always been celibate, and the ascetic life is referred to as the 'angelic life.' The *Lausiac History* by Palladius, bishop of Helenopolis (fourth/fifth century), provides many testimonies of the battles fought for the sake of virginity. Whenever a carnal thought entered the mind of Amon, for instance, he would make a piece of hot iron and lay it upon his member. Whenever the devil made an attack on Evagrius, he stood up naked the whole night long in the desert, until his flesh was quite shriveled and dried up. Demetrius, the twelfth patriarch of the Coptic Church (d. 230), made himself a eunuch of his own free will so that he was more glorious than those who were born eunuchs. Benjamin I, the thirty-eighth patriarch (623–62), dwelt in the desert and despised his body and cut off his desires for the love of Christ. Abba John, bishop of Nikiu, killed a monk of the monasteries of Scetis who had sinned with a nun, whom he had taken into the monastery. Gabriel I, the fifty-seventh patriarch (910–20), overcame the lust of sin by going around the cells of the monks to clean out their latrines, without anyone knowing about it, until his lust left him. Saint John of Armant (Kiyahk 7/December 16) was tempted by carnal thoughts, so he rolled in thorns until he was torn from head to foot and his evil imaginations were eradicated. Saint Mark the Ascetic (Hatur 10/November 19) suffered from temptations until he assumed the outward appearance of insanity and went about naked and submitted to the derision of the people.

Since the fourth century, some of the Egyptian desert fathers have endeavored to recapture the original heavenly state of paradise as well as glimpse the eschatological truth. To realize this goal they shed all worldly habits, including their garments, and lived naked, covered only with their hair, which God had provided. So as to underline their purpose of striving for a harmonious life with God's creation, these 'fools of God' sought the company of the wild beasts of the desert in fulfillment of the messianic prophecy of the heavenly state in which "the wolf shall dwell with the lamb, and the leopard shall lie down with the kid . . . and the lion shall eat straw like the ox" (Isa. 11:6–7). It was this heavenly utopia symbolized by the idyllic picture of wild beasts and dangerous reptiles in peaceful companionship with domesticated animals that inspired such naked saints as Saints Onuphrius (Ba'una 16/June 23), Timothy (Kiyahk 23/January 1), and Mary the Egyptian (Baramuda 6/April 14).

Humble submissiveness and the feeling of unworthiness motivated some hermits to leave the human society and identify themselves with the animal creation. In his travels through the inner desert in the fourth century, Saint Paphnutius (Amshir 15/February 22) met among a herd of animals a wild man whose body was covered with hair and girt with leaves, living on herbs and roots. At this sight, Paphnutius hid himself, fearing that this man was mad, but he proved to be Saint Onuphrius. Onuphrius explained that he had lived in the inner desert for sixty years without having met a person. He had found a palm tree that each year grows twelve branches, one twig for each month, quite sufficient for his bodily sustenance. His need for water was provided by a nearby spring. While the two saints conversed, an angel descended and offered them the Eucharist. After having received the divine elements, Onuphrius took leave from Paphnutius and died. Paphnutius covered Onuphrius's naked body with a piece of cloth and took him to a cave near the palm tree, which in sorrow had fallen down.

In the eighteenth century, Saint Onuphrius appeared for three consecutive nights to the abbess of the Convent of Saint Theodore in Harat al-Rum, Cairo, asking her to dig a well in the convent. This accomplished, the nuns felt that the water was bitter. The saint appeared again and advised the abbess to throw the contents of the incense box (*emshir*) into the well, and the water turned sweet. In the Chapel of Saint Onuphrius, the patron saint of the nuns, repose the relics of Saints George and Theodore, as well as those of Onuphrius.

Keeping silent was always considered one of the ascetic virtues, following the prophetic admonition, "Be silent, all flesh, before the Lord" (Zech. 2:13). Saint Pambo was one of the companions of Saint Amon in the desert of Scetis in the fourth century. He was illiterate and asked one of the brethren to teach him to recite a psalm. He was taught the first verse of Psalm 39: "I will guard my ways, that I may not sin with my tongue, I will bridle my mouth." As Pambo heard this verse, he decided to learn no more until he had been able to put this verse into practice. He remained silent for the rest of his life. In reply to Patriarch Theophilus, who visited the monks, he merely said, "If he is not edified by my silence, he will not be edified by my speech."

Clement of Alexandria (d. 215) wrote "About Laughing." He distinguished between laughter, tittering, and smiling, the latter of which he accepted. The ascetic father, following the words of Christ—"Blessed are you that weep now, for you shall laugh . . . . Woe to you that laugh now, for you shall mourn and weep" (Luke 6:21–25)—felt that laughter belonged to the heavenly future. While Jesus never laughed, he certainly wept (Luke 19:41). Repeatedly, the demons had tempted some of the desert fathers to laugh; however, they withstood the diabolic challenges, since to them laughter belonged to the passing world, which caused them to weep. Also their inability to fulfill the aim of Christian perfection led them to weep, following the psalm: "My tears have been my food day and night" (42:3).

The Equestrian Warriors
in Coptic Spirituality

THE subject of the mythological warrior who conquers the dragon—later recast as the saint conquering Satan—is as ancient as the classical Greek legends and fables. There are the victories of Zeus over Typhon, Apollo over Python, Heracles over the Hydra, and Bellerophon over the Chimera. And just as there were many heroes, there existed an abundant variety of dragons, such as those of Demeter and Athena as well as the serpents of Aesculapius and Trophonius.

Although the ancient Egyptians used to ascribe the victory over the evil Seth to Horus, it seems unlikely that the famous sandstone figure of the equestrian Horus spearing Seth (Louvre Inv. No. x 5130) lastingly inspired the medieval iconography of the popular equestrian warriors that constitute such an integral part of Coptic art and piety.

The theme of the Coptic warrior fighting Satan is actually introduced by the almost unknown Saint Sisinnios (Baramuda 26/May 4), along with his sister Alabasdria, who was overpowered by Satan (as shown in the painting in Chapel 17 in the Monastery of St. Apollo in Bawit, sixth/seventh century). It is noteworthy that from the beginning the Copts portrayed their famous warriors as equestrian fighters in spite of the fact that, as *dhimmiyin*, they were forbidden to ride on horses during most of the Islamic period. Nonetheless, the equestrian officer symbolizes the victory over the powers of evil. As such, his icon and relics are considered to possess apotropaic powers. Thus, many of the Coptic martyrs of the fourth-century persecutions have been purposely transformed into medieval equestrian saints. In the Chapel of Saint Michael in the keep of the Monastery of Saint Macarius in Wadi al-Natrun, for instance, seventeenth-century wall paintings depict the five martyrs of the family of Basilides—Eusebius (Amshir 23/March 2), Basilides (Tut 11/September 21), Justus (Amshir 10/February 17), Apoli (Misra 1/August 7), and Theoclia (Bashans 11/May 19)—as equestrian officers. In the eighteenth-century paintings in the dome of the subterranean Church of Saint Paul in the Red Sea Monastery of Saint Paul, many famous saints are shown on horseback; among them are Julius of Aqfahs (Tut 22/October 2), Apater and his sister Irene (Tut 28/October 8), Isidore, son of Bandilawus (Bashans 19/May 27), Iskhirun of Qallin (Ba'una 7/June 14), James the Sawn-Asunder (Hatur 27/December 6), and Menas (Hatur 15/November 24). Another cycle of equestrian warriors, from the fourteenth century, adorns the walls of the ancient Church of Saint Antony in the Monastery of Saint Antony.

Unquestionably, the two most popular warrior-saints among the Copts are Saint Theodore Stratelates and Saint George. However, their particular service of saving and delivering mankind from the horrors of Satan on horseback emerged only in the Middle Ages, perhaps under the influence of the Crusaders. The well-known sixth-century icon of the Holy Virgin flanked by Saints Theodore and George in the Monastery of Saint Catherine, Sinai, portrays the two warriors unmounted.

Among the popular military-saints of the Copts, Saint Theodore Stratelates precedes all others. Actually, his biography includes two characters, an original Greek and another Egyptian saint. According to the Egyptian tradition, he was born in Shutb, a village twenty kilometers south of Asyut. As an officer in the army of the emperor Licinius (308–24), he served in the war against the Persians. He was stationed in Euchaites, in eastern Anatolia. The people there worshiped a dragon that threatened the town; every year they sacrificed a small boy to feed the beast. When the son of a poor Christian widow was chosen to be thrown to the dragon, Saint Theodore appeared and killed the dragon, thereby saving the life of the boy. Later, Saint Theodore suffered martyrdom in Euchaites, which was later called Theodoropolis.

The Coptic biography of Saint George (Baramuda 23/May 1) does not mention his fight with and victory over the dragon. This means that probably during the fourteenth century the theme of the victory over the dragon was transferred from the biography of Saint Theodore Stratelates to Saint George. But it is also possible that the Copts adopted the image of the equestrian warrior Saint George overcoming the dragon from the Western Christians. The oldest version of the victory of Saint George over the dragon and his liberation of the king's daughter, who was to be sacrificed to the dragon, is found in the *Legenda aurea* by Jacobus de Voragine (c. 1263). On the northern altar screen of the Church of the Holy Virgin al-Mu'allaqa in Old Cairo, fifteen icons (1777) portray every episode of Saint George's life as described in the Coptic synaxarion, including his ministry, suffering, and martyrdom, yet there is no picture showing his victory over the dragon, because the Armenian iconographer Karapetian followed the text of the synaxarion.

The Equestrian Warrior as Deliverer

The early Christians identified "the dragon, that ancient serpent, who is the Devil and Satan" (Rev. 20:2) with the persecutions of the Christians during the reign of the emperor Domitian (A.D. 95). The Copts clearly adopted the political criteria of the beast and saw the dragon as the symbol of the Antichrist, of heresy and unbelief. Martyrs were victims of the dragon, while the doctors of the church identified theological heretics with the 'children of Satan.'

During the past few years, special attention has been focused on the various iconographical interpretations of the small figure often mounted behind the warrior-saint. In the case of Saint George, some of the most notable iconographers and scholars of medieval art were unable to identify this young lad, who holds in his right hand a coffee pot or ewer and a towel. Was he the slave or the squire of the saint? Was he the donor of the painting? Was 'he' really the princess delivered by the saint? Was he the Islamic al-Khadr, who is often identified with Saint George? Was he a Christian slave rescued from his Muslim master?

The image of the youth riding behind the warrior-saint can be traced to the post-Crusader period and appears with saints other than Saint George, but usually in different form: while the youth mounted behind Saint George is dressed in the clothes of a young Turk and holds a coffee pot and a towel, symbolizing his servant position, the youths riding behind Saints Theodore, Iskhirun, Demetrius, and Bahnam do not give the impression of being servants.

Two Coptic icons of the eighteenth and nineteenth centuries portray the theme. The icon of Saint George is the work of the Copt Ibrahim al-Nasikh and the Armenian Ohan Karapetian, dated A.M. 1469, or 1752/1753. The boy mounted behind the saint is dressed in a striped *galabiya* and holds a coffee pot in his right hand. The second icon, painted by Astasi (Eustathius) al-Rumi al-Qudsi in 1849, belongs to the Church of the Holy Virgin in Sakha, Kafr al-Shaikh, and shows the young boy dressed in a blue suit.

The Coptic warrior-saints' role as deliverers also reflects the political and social status of the Christians in the Middle East. Following the expansion of the Ottoman empire throughout the Mediterranean, Christian families lived in fear that their young boys would be compelled to join the Turkish janissaries (from *yeni chéri*, or 'new troops'). Every year a certain number of Christian youths were taken from their parents, and after undergoing a period of apprenticeship, were enrolled as *yeni chéri*. While serving their apprenticeship, the recruits were instructed in the principles of Islam. By 1826, when the janissaries were defeated by Ibrahim Aga on the *midan* of Istanbul, they numbered 135,000.

Since it was impossible for a young janissary to return to the Christian faith, the church considered him to be dead. It was this system of organized kidnapping of the Christian youth, known by the Turks as *devshirme* and by the Christians as *paidomazoma,* that the Christians reflected in their iconography of warrior-saints saving the Christian youth. It is insignificant, therefore, whether the youth riding behind the saint appears as a slave, squire, or coffee-boy. He represents the Christian youth who is delivered from the *tour-naji-bashi,* the Turkish officer who toured the provinces recruiting boys by force.

It is unlikely that many Coptic boys served as janissaries, especially since those with darker skin were excluded from the standing army. Nevertheless, it was this system that prevailed in the Ottoman empire that made the Coptic warrior-saints to be deliverers of young boys.

The Coptic iconography of Saint Theodore Stratelates always includes the son of the poor widow. He is usually shown chained to a tree. The dragon, as the 'serpent of the garden of Paradise,' is pierced with a lance.

Saint Iskhirun of Qallin appears sometimes as a double of Saint George, even though his biography mentions neither a fight with a dragon or serpent nor the rescue of a youth. Saint Iskhirun suffered martyrdom at the hands of the governor Arianus in Upper Egypt. Apparently eighteenth-century Coptic iconographers like Ibrahim al-Nasikh transferred some of the characteristics of Saint George, such as the white horse, the triumph over the dragon, and the coffee boy, to Saint Iskhirun of Qallin.

The popular veneration of the warrior-saints among the Copts is unsurpassed. In 1980 there were 350 Coptic churches dedicated to Saint George and twenty-three named after Saint Theodore. Undoubtedly, within the past twenty years this number has grown significantly, both in Egypt and in the diaspora, as the overall number of churches has grown. Moreover, almost all Coptic churches have multiple altars, one of which is usually dedicated to either Saint George or Saint Theodore Stratelates.

Not surprisingly, some of the most popular pilgrimages are to the churches and monasteries dedicated to Saint George. The best-known of these are:

Mit Damsis, Gharbiya, Misra 17–25/August 23–31
Birma, near Tanta, Ba'una 3/June 10
Mahalla Marhum, near Tanta, in Abib/July

Tukh al-Nasara, Shibin al-Kom, Baramuda 19–26/April 27–May 4
Minya al-Qamh, Sharqiya, in Abib/July
Kafr Ayyub, south of Minya al-Qamh, Abib 11–18/July 18–25
Shubra, Cairo, in Tut/September
Greek Orthodox Panegyris, Old Cairo, Baramuda 15/April 23
Sidmant al-Gabal, south of Madinat al-Fayyum, Ascension
Biba, south of Beni Suef, one week after Ascension
Bani Murr, Abnub, Baramuda 23/May 1
Dair al-'Awana, al-Badari, Hatur 7/November 16
Dair al-Hadid, Akhmim, Hatur 7/November 16 and Ascension
Dair Mari Girgis, Dimuqrat, Hatur 1–7/November 10–17

Two pilgrimages are dedicated to Saint Theodore Stratelates:

Dair al-Sanquriya, Bani Mazar, Ascension
Dair Amir Tadrus (the Convent of Saint Theodore the Warrior),
    Madinat Habu, Tuba 16/January 24

On the occasion of the pilgrimage, Copts often have a symbol of the Christian faith tattooed on the inside of their right wrist. In many instances, the chosen design is the equestrian warrior-saint with the small boy mounted behind him and holding a coffee pot. This shows the obvious popularity that this theme has acquired in the spirituality of the Copts.

The veneration of the saints' relics is part of the pilgrimage. The relics are normally kept in cylindrical bolsters covered with precious dark-red silk or velvet. They repose beneath the icon of the saint. In the first inventory of Coptic relics by the Alexandrian deacon Mawhub ibn Mufarrag al-Iskandarani at the time of Pope Cyril II (1078–92), the relics of Saint George reposed in Lydda in Palestine. Three hundred years later, they were venerated in the Church of Saint George in Birma, near Tanta. During the patriarchate of Matthew I (1378–1408), they were transferred to the Monastery of Saint Samuel at al-Qalamun, south of the Fayyum. A few years later, in the days of Pope Gabriel V (1409–27), they were moved again, to the Church of Saint George in Old Cairo (Ba'una 3/June 10), where they were the cause of many miracles. In my 1999 inventory of Coptic relics, I listed eighteen Saint George reliquaries and five Saint Theodore reliquaries. These figures are incomplete, on account of the practice of dividing and distributing relics to other churches in Egypt and in the diaspora.

The 'Silverless' Physicians
in Coptic Spirituality

❦❧❦❧

Gods and Saints as Healers

FROM time immemorial, the physically and mentally ill have turned to God, the gods, or their intermediaries for help and healing. This is understandable, for according to primitive religious attitudes, diseases were regarded as divine punishment for any violation of moral or ritual laws. Thus, for example, Uzziah was stricken with leprosy because he burned incense for the Lord, even though he was not of the consecrated sons of Aaron (2 Chron. 26:16–21). In fact, throughout the ancient world and today's traditional societies, religion, magic, and medicine have been and still are deeply interwoven.

In ancient Egypt, all diseases except those of the eyes were handled by members of a specialized clergy, the priests of the goddess Sekhmet, who had their own rule and hierarchy. Sekhmet, the lion-headed deity, inflicted men with diseases, but she also healed their sufferings. The ancient Egyptians addressed their prayers to different gods, and never designated, as the Greeks did with Aesculapius, a single god of medicine. Other healing gods included Thoth, who was represented either as a monkey or as a person with an ibis head surmounted by the solar disc or the lunar crescent and whom the Greeks later identified with Hermes Trismegistos. There was also Horus, and Thoueris, the hippopotamus-shaped goddess, who presided over childbirth and was invoked as the 'good nurse.'

With the christianization of the ancient world, the pre-Christian gods were overthrown and their priests were forced to either convert or surrender their healing practices. But instead of ruthlessly abolishing the pagans' religious-magical healing ministry, the Christians succeeded in transforming the temples and shrines into churches and cathedrals, in which the healing cults survived the religious change. One of the best-known examples is the transformation of the Serapeum of Canopus in Abuqir, which was destroyed in 391 by the fanatic patriarch Theophilus, into the shrine of Saints Cyrus and John, the two brothers of Damanhur who became the most popular *anargyroi,* or silverless physicians, of the Egyptian Christians in Alexandria and Lower Egypt.

Instead of the fourteen 'Helpers in Need' of the Roman Catholic Church and the twelve 'silverless' physicians of the Byzantine churches, the Copts know of only five doctor-saints whom they call on in times of sickness. These physicians used to treat their patients without payment, thereby following the word of the Lord: "Heal the sick, raise the dead, cleanse lepers, cast out demons. You received without pay, give without pay" (Matt. 10:8). Those physicians who answered this call earned the name of 'silverless' doctors, or *anargyroi.*

Saints Cyrus and John

Following the suspension of the healing cult in the Serapeum of Canopus in 391, the patriarch Cyril I transferred the relics of the two physicians Cyrus and John to the Church of Saint Mark. The established therapeutic practice of 'incubation,' in which the afflicted spend hours or days in the presence of the relics, was retained. Many reports of miracles due to the influence of the relics of the two physicians made this church one of the most desirable pilgrimage resorts through the ninth century. The Greek Orthodox patriarch Sophronios I of Alexandria (830–50) was healed from his eye infection at the church in Abuqir.

Around the tenth century, the relics of the two saints were transferred to Old Cairo, where they reposed in the Coptic Church of Saints Cyrus and John within the Qasr al-Sham'. In the eleventh century, however, this church received the relics of Saint Barbara, which then determined the patronage and popularity of the church. Today, some of the relics of the two physicians are still venerated in a newer Church of Saints Cyrus and John south of Qasr al-Sham' in Old Cairo, and in a small church dedicated to the two physicians which was built in Abuqir in 1935. The ancient healing cult associated with the once famous 'silverless' physicians Cyrus and John seems to be extinct in Egypt. Relics of the two physicians are venerated in several Greek monasteries on Mount Athos, in the Hagia Lavra in Kalavrita, and in the Monastery of Saint John on Patmos.

The Immaculata of 1830

*The Apparition of the Holy Virgin
at Zaytun, 1968: the souvenir
'official' picture*

*The Apparition of the Holy Virgin at
Ard Baba Dublu, Shubra, 1986:
the souvenir card*

The blood-weeping Mater Dolorosa in the Church of Saint George, Wadi al-Natrun

The Nativity of Christ, with Saint Joseph, twelfth/thirteenth century (Codex Copte 13, Paris)

The Twenty-four Elders of the Apocalypse, Coptic Museum, Cairo

Saint Theodore with the youth mounted behind him, by Ibrahim al-Nasikh and Ohan Karapetian, eighteenth century

Saint George and the youth with the coffeepot, by Astasi al-Rumi, Church of the Holy Virgin, Sakha

Tenth-century reliquary, Monastery of the Syrians, Wadi al-Natrun

Saint Marina with the child, Church of the Holy Virgin, Harat al-Rum

Saint Antony the Great, by Father Yusab al-Rayyani, 1989

The relics of Saints Dioscorus and Aesclepius, Church of Saint Shenuda, Old Cairo

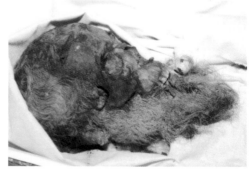

One of the Martyrs of Naqlun, Monastery of Saint Gabriel, Fayyum

Saint Bashnuna, Church of Saints Sergius and Bacchus, Old Cairo

Saint Simeon, the one-eyed tanner, Church of Saint Simeon, Muqattam, Cairo

The Flight of the Holy Family, by Youssef Nassif and Boudour Latif

The Flight of the Holy Family, by Astasi al-Rumi, Church of Saints Sergius and Bacchus, Old Cairo

The Chains of Saint George, Convent of Saint George, Old Cairo

The Chains of Saint George at the Church of Saint George, Jerusalem

Christ's footprint, Church of the Holy Virgin, Sakha (photograph by Norbert Schiller)

Saints Cosmas and Damian

On the west bank of the Nile, between Giza and al-Badrashayn, is the village of Manyal Shiha. The Church of Saints Cosmas and Damian, two other famous 'silverless' physicians, is situated in the western part of the village. Annually on Ba'una 20–22 (June 27–29), many patients from Lower and Upper Egypt suffering from nervous disorders and epilepsy visit this church in hopes of being healed of their afflictions. The cult of the two saints can be traced to the fifth century; the oldest iconographical representation of the two physicians, in a mosaic in the dome of the Church of Saint George in Thessaloniki, dates from around the year 400. Some scholars have suggested that the cult of the two doctors was somehow related to the widespread veneration of the popular Dioscuri, Castor and Polydeuces, whose temple in Constantinople was situated near the Church of Saints Cosmas and Damian. Throughout Egypt, especially in Upper Egypt, the cult of Saints Cosmas and Damian and their mother and three brothers was well established. One of the earliest Egyptian testimonies to these saints is a seventh-century wall painting from the former Monastery of Wadi Sarga south of Asyut, now in the British Museum in London. This painting shows the two physicians carrying their medical instruments in triangular handbags. Between them are their brothers Anthimus, Leontius, and Euprepius. In the square inset between the two physicians are the three youths Ananias, Azarias, and Misail in the fire with the Angel of God (Dan. 3). Other early wall paintings of the two physicians were in Chapel 18 of the Monastery of Apollo at Bawit and in Dair Abu Hinnis, south of Shaikh 'Abada. An altar of Saints Cosmas and Damian was consecrated in 1177 in the Church of Saint Victor in the region of al-Habash in Old Cairo. Furthermore, churches dedicated to the two physicians existed in the twelfth century in Itfih, twenty kilometers south of al-Saff, and in Qus, south of Qina.

The Church of Saints Cosmas and Damian in Manyal Shiha was restored in the twelfth century. Today, the relics of Saints Cosmas and Damian repose in a new shrine on the south wall of the choir. It is noteworthy that the Coptic iconography shows the two physicians in their Byzantine habits. Since they were not Egyptians, they were believed to be from the 'Byzantine world,' though they were originally from Arabia (from Dabarma). Coptic art hesitated to portray 'Arab saints.'

The relics of the two saints are still very popular outside of Egypt as well, if one considers that in Greek churches and monasteries alone there repose a total of eighty-two relics of Saint Cosmas and seventy-four of Saint Damian. Their skulls are shown in the cathedrals of Essen and Hildesheim in Germany.

Saint Colluthus

According to the Coptic synaxarion for Bashans 25 (June 2), Colluthus was the son of Heralamon, a distinguished citizen of Antinoë (now Shaikh 'Abada). Through his friendship with Philip, the son of Bishop Abadiun of Antinoë, the young Colluthus was led to the study of philosophy and medicine. When they became physicians, the two young men refused to accept any remuneration for their services, and thus they became known as *anargyroi.*

When the governor, Arianus, visited Antinoë, he was so impressed with the handsomeness and gracious personality of Colluthus that he determined to seek a wife from his kindred, and so become the doctor's brother-in-law. Colluthus, however, abandoned his wealth and adopted the ascetic life. In 304, early in the Diocletian persecutions, he was arrested and sent to prison. His relationship with the governor saved him from being executed until Arianus was replaced. He was questioned, and finally suffered martyrdom.

The cult of Saint Colluthus must have emerged soon after his martyrdom, for by the middle of the sixth century, Phoebammon, bishop of Akhmin and diadochos for all Egypt during the exile of the patriarch Theodosius I (536–67), delivered an encomium for Saint Colluthus on the occasion of the dedication of a church to the martyr in the iniquitous village of Pneuit, "which is the land of Sodom."

Whereas from the sixth to the eleventh century the cult of the *anargyros* Colluthus centered around his native town of Antinoë, there is good evidence that by the twelfth century or even later, the cult center was transferred to the vicinity of Asyut, where Abu al-Makarim recorded Colluthus' relics. This assumption is substantiated by the account of al-Maqrizi, the fifteenth-century Islamic topographer and historian, who stated that a *mulid,* or birthday celebration, in honor of the *anargyros* was held in the district of Rifah al-Gharbi in the province of Asyut. Moreover, he added that in the Church of Saint Colluthus, "who was a physician and a monk, wonderful cures from eye diseases were performed." Inflammation of the eyes was a very common disease among the villagers of the Nile Valley, and it is interesting to note that a Cairo Medical Papyrus includes a recipe for the treatment for ophthalmia which is ascribed to Saint Colluthus.

A cult honoring Saint Colluthus is practiced to this day in the village of al-Fant, on the west bank of the Nile between al-Fashn and Maghagha. In the center of the village is the Church of Apa Klog, to whom the villagers ascribe numerous miracles. The Copts of al-Fant gather in the church twice a year, on Ba'una 20 (June 27) and Tuba 20 (January 28). According to local tradition, 'their' Colluthus, son of Dioscorus and Euphemia, was born in al-Fant in the third century. At the age of twelve he had memorized all of the books of the New Testament and the Psalms except for the Apocalypse. His ministry included healing wounds caused by snakes and scorpions, and he raised the son of the governor Arianus from the dead. Against his will he was ordained to the priesthood. On account of his Christian testimony, he suffered martyrdom in 304. The villagers maintain that he received three crowns, for his chastity, asceticism, and martyrdom.

The Women Saints in Coptic Spirituality

☙✦☙✦☙

THE positions and roles of women in the Coptic Church are largely determined by the testimonies of the Holy Scriptures and those of the church
fathers. Like all churches of apostolic origin, the Coptic Church prohibits
women from assuming any priestly or sacramental functions. On account of
the widespread ordinations of women as pastors and bishops in Western
churches (Anglican, Evangelical, and Old Catholic) since the middle of the
twentieth century, Pope Shenuda III has repeatedly declared the irrevocable
and incontestable teaching of the church, which prohibits women from carrying out priestly offices.

This position is based on Paul's statements: "As in all the churches of the
saints, the women should keep silence in the churches. For they are not permitted to speak, but should be subordinate, as even the law says" (1 Cor.
14:33–34), and "I permit no woman to teach or to have authority over men;
she is to keep silent" (1 Tim. 2:12). It was also Eve's disobedience (Gen. 3:6;
1 Tim. 2:14) that prohibits a woman from engaging in any form of a priestly office, and when a woman is in a state of "ritual impurity" (Lev 15:19–25),
she must not even approach the altar, not to mention take the Eucharist.
With respect to the status of women, the Old Testament ritual impurity laws
were fully accepted by the fathers of the early church. The second canon of
Saint Dionysius of Alexandria (d. 264) clearly admonishes "menstruous
women not to approach the Holy Table or to touch the body and blood of
Christ." Timothy I, pope of Alexandria (378–84), wrote the "Questions and
Answers," the seventh of which asks, "If a woman finds herself in the plight
peculiar to her sex, ought she to come to the Mysteries on that day?"
Timothy's answer was short: "She ought not to do so, until she has been puri-
fied." The same laws were repeated in the Middle Ages by Pope Cyril III
(1235–43), and they apply to this day. Also, following the delivery of a boy,
the mother must refrain from attending church for forty days, and in the case
of the delivery of a girl, she must stay away for eighty days!

These laws and prescriptions have made it extremely difficult for women to serve their Lord through the regular and established channels of the church. It is understandable, therefore, that some women discovered strange and unusual methods and means to fulfill their religious inclinations.

The Women Monks

In 1945 the remains of an extraordinary Coptic library were discovered in a ruined tomb near Nag' Hammadi in Upper Egypt. Among these thirteen leather-bound papyrus volumes was the Gospel of Thomas, an anthology of 144 "Sayings of Jesus." Scholars have assigned these sayings, or *logia,* to the middle of the second century. The last of these sayings (114) quotes Peter: "Let Mary go out from among us, because women are not worthy of the Life." In answer, Jesus said, "See, I shall lead her, so that I will make her male, that she too may become a living spirit, resembling you males. For every woman who makes herself male will enter the Kingdom of Heaven." Was it possible that some of the numerous Coptic women of the fourth through seventh centuries who disguised themselves as monks could have been following these sayings of their Lord? In that case, their reactions would be fully understandable, for the truly faithful at that time would happily don the habit of a monk in hopes of attaining eternal life.

The biographies of the women monks are quite similar. They were usually daughters of Roman emperors, kings, governors, or notables. Influenced and inspired by the asceticism of the Egyptian desert fathers, the young women assumed the disguise of a courier, in the case of Hilaria, or they escaped from marriage proposals by donning male attire, as Apollinaria did. As monks—often described as eunuchs—they entered the desert of Scetis or Wadi al-Natrun. There they lived as hermits, each inhabiting a cell under the direction of a father. Because of their asceticism, which often surpassed that of the other monks, they became known for their charismata of healing and exorcism.

Saint Hilaria (Tuba 21/January 29), daughter of the emperor Zeno, is venerated today by the nuns of the Convent of Saint George in Old Cairo, where a shrine commemorates 'Hilary the Eunuch,' so called because she had no beard. Saint Marina (Misra 15/August 21) suffered from a false charge of paternity. She assumed male attire and joined a monastery, where she was known as Marinus. Once she was sent out on business and had to pass the night in an inn. There a soldier had relations with the innkeeper's daughter but advised her to lay the blame on the monk Marinus, which she did. The innkeeper's daughter bore a son, and the soldier took the child to Marinus for support, which she accepted. Expelled from her monastery, Marina cared for the infant, who eventually became a monk. After Marina died, the secret of her sex was discovered, and her innocence was established. She is commemorated especially in the Church of the Holy Virgin in Harat al-Rum in Cairo. Another woman monk was Theodora (Tut 11/September 21), who lived as Theodorus, with her son as servant, in a Coptic monastery. Because of her strict asceticism, she was eventually admitted as a monk. Only after her death was her sex discovered. Pelagia (Baba 11/October 21) was a woman monk in the desert of Scetis, where she was associated with the famous Abba Daniel of Scetis (485–580). Matruna (Hatur 14/November 23) lived as a monk in the seventh century in the inner desert, where John the Hegumen discovered her. Anastasia (Tuba 26/February 3) was asked to marry the emperor Justin I (518–27), but she fled to Egypt, assumed male attire, and found refuge with Abba Daniel of Scetis. Save the abbot, no one else knew her secret, which was discovered after she died. Apollinaria is said to have been the daughter of the Western Roman emperor Anthemius (467–72). She escaped from the court and, disguised as a monk, entered the desert of Scetis. In the Greek Orthodox Church, she is commemorated on January 5. Her vita seems to be a variant of the story of Hilaria.

This practice reached such proportions that by the late fourth century, the members of the ecumenical Synod of Gangra in Paphlagonia (Canon XIII) decided to anathematize those women who assumed male attire to pass as monks.

The Virgins

The Coptic Catechism, drawing on the lessons in chapter 7 of 1 Corinthians, clearly states that "those who vow celibacy, and are able to keep their vows, have a more excellent way and a more perfect holiness. For marriage is holy, but celibacy is better and holier."

Throughout the early history of the Coptic Church, dedicated virgins have played an important role in the ascetic movement, and the church now commemorates twenty-two holy virgins who are models of chastity and devotion. While Saint Antony is generally regarded as the 'father of Christian monks,' with the same justification Saint Syncletica should be called the 'mother of Christian nuns,' the role model for those women who voluntarily relinquished this world to dedicate their lives to God. According to Athanasius I, the twentieth pope of Alexandria, her biographer, Saint Syncletica grew up in an aristocratic home in Alexandria. As a young woman, she had already decided to live a God-fearing life, maintaining fasts and vigils at her parental home. Following the death of her parents, she sold her inheritance and distributed it among the poor. She left the opulent home and withdrew to the desert, where other virgins gathered around her and she taught them the divine virtues of asceticism. Saint Syncletica reached the age of eighty unaffected by her fasts and vigils. Three days before her death, she saw a vision of angels, who invited her to follow in their train.

Another woman saint of the early monastic period was Saint Talida, the founder of a convent in Antinoë, in the Fayyum. There sixty nuns lived under her guidance. One of the rules of Saint Talida's convent was that its gates were never to be locked, so it could be a place of refuge day and night. Saint Talida spent eighty years as a nun and died at a ripe old age. Long is the list of other women who for one reason or another had embraced the ascetic life, sometimes to atone for their sins, sometimes to express their gratitude for the goodness of the Lord. Alexandra (Amshir 7/February 14) lived for twelve years locked in a tomb, thereby hoping to atone for a frivolous life. Athanasia (Misra 2/August 8) had operated a house of ill repute but later lived a life of penance as a desert hermit. Mary the Alexandrian (Tuba 24/February 1) was the daughter of noble parents. For fifteen years she lived in a convent before she became a hermit in the inner desert. Martha of Egypt (Ba'una 3/June 10) had lived a dissolute life. As a penitent she entered a convent, where she remained for twenty-five years. Theodora (Baramuda 11/April 19; 395–412) was an ascetic in Alexandria and the author of some of the sayings cited in the Apophthegmata, a collection of sayings of the Fathers of Scetis with anecdotes. The first translatons of such a collection appear about the end of the fourth century; the existing collection, however, is not earlier than the end of the fifth. It was originally compiled in Greek and afterward translated into Sa'idic.

Saint Pachomius (d. 349), the founder of organized monastic life in Upper Egypt, established nine monasteries for monks and two convents for nuns. Mary, his sister, became the first nun in the convent he built near his monastery in Tabennesi. Rules for cooperation between the monks and the nuns were laid down: if the nuns needed new cells, the brethren built them; if the brethren needed new clothes, the sisters sewed them.

The religious renewal in the Coptic Church, which had its beginnings in the second half of the twentieth century, led also to a revival of the ascetic life among women. Contemplative nuns had lived in the context of the church ever since the days of Saint Pachomius, but during the patriarchate of Cyril VI (1959–71) and Shenuda III (1971–), new forms of religious life for Coptic women emerged. By 1965 Bishop Athanasius of Beni Suef and al-Bahnasa had instituted the Daughters of Saint Mary (Banat Maryam), a community for women that combined the monastic life with the social aspects of

Christian service. These women work in the educational and medical fields. In addition to these socially active nuns, Pope Shenuda III initiated toward the end of the 1970s the 'consecrated women' (*mukarrasat*), as a step to the officially recognized deaconesses. These 'consecrated women' received their ecclesiastical acceptance in 1992 and now serve in dioceses and parishes all over Egypt. Also, the number of contemplative nuns in Cairo, the Delta, and Upper Egypt has significantly increased. Today, more than five hundred contemplative nuns serve in the nine Coptic convents. In the late 1970s, Pope Shenuda III decreed that the contemplative nuns, like all Coptic monks, were to wear a skullcap, the *qalansuwa*, the most prominent symbol of the revival of the Coptic monastic movement. According to tradition, the *qalansuwa*, a cap divided into two halves with six crosses embroidered on each half, was first worn by Saint Antony. In one of his struggles with the devil, Saint Antony's cap was torn in two halves. So as to be constantly aware of the powers of the evil one, all Coptic monks and nuns now wear the *qalansuwa*.

The Mothers

The sacrament of marriage is a legal bond between the bridegroom and his bride, sanctified by the grace of the Holy Spirit for the attainment of the lawful benefits, which are the mutual aid in making a livelihood and seeking pure seed. In the Book of Genesis it is stated, "Then the Lord God said: 'It is not good that the man should be alone; I will make him a helper fit for him'" (2:18), and "Therefore a man leaves his father and his mother and cleaves to his wife, and they become one flesh" (2:24). Abraham and his family are promised several times a posterity as numerous as the stars (15:5) or "the sand which is on the seashore" (22:17).

The New Testament reaffirms the sacredness of the marital relationship (Matt. 19:4–6, Mark 10:7–8). Jesus performed his first miracle at a wedding feast at Cana in Galilee (John 2:1–11), and adopted the image of the bridegroom to explain the joy of the Christian (Mark 2:19–20, Matt. 25:1–12, John 3:29). The same apostle who praised virginity so highly also provides us with the most profound text for the doctrine of the sacredness of marriage. In the Epistle to the Ephesians, the marital unity of husband and wife is compared to the unity of Christ to his church. As the church is related to Christ, its head, in the subordination of devotion and love, so too the wife's subordination to her husband, and as Christ loves his church, so a husband should nourish and cherish his own flesh (Eph. 5:24–33).

The Coptic synaxarion lists a total of eighteen mothers and their children who suffered martyrdom during the pre-Nicene persecutions. Among the more popular mothers are Armada and her children, Armanius and Amah (Ba'una 8/June 15). Theodota was the mother of five children, among them the two 'silverless' physicians Cyrus and John (Hatur 22/December 1). A nineteenth-century icon of the family adorns the walls of the Church of the Holy Virgin al-Mu'allaqa in Old Cairo.

In three cases, the Coptic Church has institutionalized the 'mother and child' martyrdoms through popular pilgrimages. In Esna on Kiyahk 14 (December 23), the nuns of the Convent of Saint Ammonius venerate the martyrdom of Saint Dulagi and her four sons, Surus, Harman, Banufa, and Shatayasi. In the Upper Egyptian episcopal city of Tahta, the Copts gather in the local cathedral on Abib 15 (July 22) to venerate their patron saints, Julietta and her young son Cyriacus, who suffered martyrdom in the fourth century. One of the popular pilgrimages in the Nile Delta honors Saint Rebecca and her five children and takes place in conjunction with the large Saint George pilgrimage on Misra 16 (August 22). Many pilgrims from Mit Damsis cross the Damietta branch of the Nile and proceed to the Church of Saint Rebecca at Sunbat, which holds the relics of the mother and her children, Agathon, Peter, John, Amon, and Amona (Abib 8/July 15). Another pilgrimage has been recently initiated to the shrine of Saint Mohrail and her little brother Hor (Tuba 14/January 22) in the Church of Saints Cosmas and Damian in Manyal Shiha, south of Giza.

The renewed interest in the veneration of mother saints has a parallel in the church's social work, in the form of educational agencies on both the parish and diocesan levels that help mothers and children.

Recently Discovered Martyrs

᪣᪢᪣

THE observant and attentive visitor to the Coptic Orthodox churches in the various cities, towns, and provinces of Egypt and in the diaspora must notice the recent widespread dissemination of relics. According to the local clergy, they belong either to the so-called Fayyum martyrs or to the Akhmim martyrs, the remains of which were discovered in the two regions in 1990 and 1991, in one case by accident, and in the other through an excavation project.

In both cases the mummified remains were unearthed and subsequently dispatched to the bishopric of Fayyum and Akhmim and from there to numerous dioceses and parishes for veneration. The churches that have these relics keep them in small, octagonal tubes covered with some precious textile. They repose in the choir on a table or in a specially constructed reliquary. The standard response to an inquiry about the identity of those recent acquisitions is that they belong to the martyrs of the early persecutions, meaning those of the period of Diocletian and his colleague Maximian.

What is the reason for the sudden interest in the relics of relatively unknown martyrs? Furthermore, what is the purpose of the dissemination of ecclesiastical reminiscences of events that are said to have occurred 1,600 years ago? In an age in which the Western churches have practically abolished the veneration of the relics of their saints, the Coptic Church seems to be resuscitating a medieval cult. What is to be gained from this reflection on a rather distant past?

History does repeat itself! In 1578 the ancient Roman Via Salaria collapsed, thereby giving access to the famous Roman catacombs and the subsequent widespread export of relics of notable persons whose names are even mentioned in the Epistles of Paul. The discovery provided welcome spiritual support for the Tridentine Counter-Reformation; likewise, the discovery and almost global distribution of the relics of the Fayyum and Akhmim martyrs in 1990 and 1991 has offered an additional 'historical dimension' to the present renaissance of the Coptic Church.

Akhmim, City of Martyrs

The persecutions of the Christians during the reign of Diocletian and Maximian resulted in the largest number of martyrs in a short period. In Upper Egypt the persecutions were carried out by the governor Arianus, who had come from Lycopolis (Asyut) to hunt for Christians in the provinces of Panopolis (Akhmim) and Antaiopolis (Qaw al-Kabir). His arrival in Akhmim is commemorated by the Copts on Kiyahk 30 (January 8). The Vatican recension of the Coptic synaxarion for Tuba 1 (January 9) mentions 8,140 Christians who refused to offer sacrifices to the Roman gods and subsequently suffered martyrdom in Akhmim. Whereas most of the Akhmim martyrs remained anonymous, some of them receive special commemoration. Dioscorus and Aesculapius (Tuba 1) were ascetics in the desert east of Akhmim when Saint Michael appeared to them and ordered them to bear witness before Arianus. They were tortured and finally beheaded. Forty soldiers of the garrison, along with their captains, Philemon and Akourius, joined the saints in their martyrdom. Both Ananias and Khouzi of Akhmim laid down their lives for Christ and are commemorated on Kiyahk 16 (December 25).

However, not only the Romans persecuted the Christians. Mercurius and Ephraem (Abib 30/August 6), natives of Akhmim, were monks in the Thebaid and suffered martyrdom during the reign of the Arian emperor Constantius II (337–61) because they upheld the orthodox faith. Menas the 'new martyr' (Amshir 17/February 24) lived in the seventh century as a hermit near one of the monasteries east of Akhmim. He went to Hermopolis Magna (al-Ashmunain), where the Arabs killed him.

The Monastery of the Martyrs

On a ridge at the edge of the desert east of al-Hawawish, six kilometers northeast of Akhmim, are three monasteries: the northern one near al-Salamuni is dedicated to the archangel Michael, the central one is the Monastery of the Martyrs (Dair al-Shuhada'), and the southern one is dedicated to the Holy Virgin.

The present buildings of the Monastery of the Martyrs date to the eighteenth and nineteenth centuries. This is substantiated by the iconographic and calligraphic testimonies on the walls of the altar rooms. In 1740 Richard Pococke mentioned that the monastery was inhabited. In 1889, according to U. Bouriant, only one priest lived there. Since 1989 the monastery has been occupied by one monk. The chancel screen of the altar of the martyrs has an inlaid Coptic text that reads, "Be greeted, Church, thou mansion of angels."

The Necropolis East of Akhmim

Dair al-Shuhada' was built within a large necropolis that contains tombs from a number of periods. According to the statement by Abuna Ghubriyal al-Antuni of the Monastery of the Martyrs, a large number of mummies were discovered in March 1990 as the monk was clearing some tombs near the monastery to prepare an olive orchard.

The modern history of this necropolis begins with the reports about this vast burial site by such European travelers as Paul Lucas (1714), Richard Pococke, W. G. Browne (1797), M. Saint-Gènis (1798), and N. L'Hôte (1839). Their impressions of the necropolis are certainly informative as to the historical and geographical extent of the site.

It was in March 1884 that G. Maspero and Schiaparelli entrusted the excavations of the necropolis east of Akhmim to the Ra'is Ghalib of al-Qurna (Thebes), who gave the actual work of digging to the local soldiery. Moreover, a number of licenses for digging in the necropolis were given to certain citizens of Akhmim. Maspero records that in a short time as many as ten thousand mummies were unearthed, "mais la plupart sans valeur." Many mummies were subsequently sold to the Egyptian Railway as fuel for the engines; others were purchased by American paper mills. Between the years 1884 and 1888, the necropolis was thoroughly despoiled. In 1889 U. Bouriant described the devastations and destructions: "Aujourd'hui c'est une véritable pillage qu'il est impossible de réprimer. Tout est bouleversé, arraché brisé . . . la nécropole copte, c'est une nécropole finie . . . ." In 1895 R. Forrer visited the necropolis: "As far as you can see, there are black holes, cavities, where tombs were opened, other black spots are bodies, mummies that were robbed of their textiles . . . everywhere the necropolis has been systematically plundered." Nonetheless, here and there some mummies and fragments of bones escaped the search of the late-nineteenth-century 'excavators.' The history of the plunder of the necropolis is described in detail by Klaus P. Kuhlmann of the German Archaeological Institute in Cairo.

The Martyrs of the Fayyum

The Monastery of Saint Gabriel, also known as Dair Abu Khashab or Dair Malak Ghubriyal, is a traditional pilgrimage site in Naqlun on the southeastern border of the Fayyum oasis near Qalamshah. During the summer of 1991, the Coptic diocese of the Fayyum was restoring and expanding the pilgrimage center. At the same time, the Egyptian Antiquities Organization (EAO) and the Polish Center of Archaeology in Cairo were excavating in the proximity of the monastery, studying especially the layout and architecture of the early Christian laura of Naqlun. In the course of the excavations, three caskets, each containing four mummies, were discovered and unearthed about 150 meters southwest of the monastery compound. Without much effort, the three caskets were transferred to the Church of Saint Gabriel within the monastery. They were placed in the southern aisle of the nave and covered with new white linen sheets. Moreover, the mummies were photographed for a seven-page folder with twelve colored pictures to be sold for local pilgrims at the monastery kiosk. On account of the obvious marks of torture—some bodies appeared to have been strangled, while others showed marks from an axe or hatchet—the church declared them martyrs of the Christian faith.

Today the monastery is occupied and being served by twelve monks. Regular services are held for the Christians of the region. At the time of the annual *mulid* in honor of the archangel Gabriel, large numbers of Coptic pilgrims from the Fayyum and Beni Suef assemble at the monastery and inhabit the many new dwelling places around the church. Since 1991 the team of the Polish Center of Archaeology in Cairo under Professor Godlewski has restored the medieval wall paintings in the Church of Saint Gabriel.

The Identification and Dating of the Coptic Mummies

Attempts to pinpoint the identity of the assassinated persons, the tragic and violent circumstances of their death, and the date of the massacre have led to different conclusions. At this stage, various data shall be presented with the understanding that they constitute merely a preliminary report.

I suggest the politically unstable weeks and months in October and November 1798. Witnesses report marauding, looting, and plundering groups of Mamluks in this particular region. These may have massacred the Christian *fellahin* who had sought refuge within the monastery compound. At this time, the monastery was partially destroyed and probably deserted. It served merely as pilgrimage center for annual *mawalid*. Under these circumstances, the monastic buildings, situated in the desert only a few kilometers from the fertile land, could have been an ideal refuge from the extortions, confiscations, and plunderings of the roving gangs of Mamluks.

Following the battle of Sidmant al-Gabal on October 7, 1798, the victorious French forces under General Louis C.-A. Desaix de Veygoux withdrew to al-Lahun, about ten kilometers east of Dair Malak Ghubriyal. Later they camped in the northeastern section of the Fayyum, in the villages of Saila, Sirsina, al-Rawda, and al-Rub'iyat, east of Sinnuris. This means that the French troops never approached the vicinity of the monastery, neither prior to nor following the battle.

The fact that marauding Mamluks terrorized, plundered, and killed the *fellahin* is sufficiently documented. These actions were referred to merely as 'organizing,' and villagers were subjected to severe extortion and taxation. The presence of Mamluk bands in the proximity of Naqlun is mentioned in the report by General Desaix. The manner in which these Mamluks dealt with the villagers, especially the Copts, is described by Vivant Denon, who was an eyewitness: "South of Minya, the Mamluks demanded from the Copts one hundred camels. Because they were unable to satisfy their demands, sixty Copts were killed. The Christians were so angered that they killed eight Mamluks."

Should one accept the provisional dating of Professor Godlewski and my own impressions and perceptions about the mummies, the massacre of Naqlun may well have occurred during the chaotic situations in the region during the days of October/ November 1798. However, many Copts believe the martyrs belong to an earlier date, and some scientific analysis supports this.

On December 29, 1991, I visited Dair Malak Ghubriyal, where I met with Abuna Yoel al-Bishoi and Abuna 'Abd al-Masih al-Buli. With absolute certainty, Abuna Yoel explained that the mummies were Coptic martyrs who were killed by Muslims, after suffering severe violence and torture, in or around the thirteenth century. To verify this data, Abuna Yoel gave me a 10-by-15-centimeter dark-green linen fragment of a mummy's shroud that had been subjected to a carbon-14 analysis in Europe. In the spring of 1992 I submitted the linen sample to the Institute for Radiocarbon Dating of Lower Saxony in Hanover for a carbon-14 test. The result was a date between 1260 and 1385.

In a letter dated February 10, 1992, Anba Abra'am, bishop of the Fayyum, wrote to me: "The relics of the martyrs in Dair al-Malak Ghobrial, Naqlun, were analyzed, and they proved to go back to the twelfth century." This information was sent to me several months prior to the receipt of the results of the radiocarbon examination. Upon my questioning, Dr. Gawdat Gabra, director of the Coptic Museum in Old Cairo, assured me that he had been unable to receive a reasonable and scientific reply to his inquires about the so-called martyrs of Naqlun. He denied that a scientific testing of the mummies had been carried out.

Should we accept the dates of the carbon-14 examination of the linen fragment for the massacre of Naqlun, namely the period between 1260 and 1385, several violent situations could be suggested. During these years, Egypt was ruled by twenty-five Bahri Mamluk sultans. At the same time, twelve Coptic patriarchs occupied the throne of Saint Mark. The life of the

Christians was largely characterized by political and economic insecurity as well as periodic raids and the destruction of churches. Al-Maqrizi records the severe persecutions of the Christians in 1320–21 by the Bahri Mamluk al-Malik al-Nasir Muhammad during the patriarchate of John IX (1320–27). More than fifty-five churches and monasteries were destroyed, and many Christians suffered martyrdom. Therefore, the massacre of Naqlun may have been part of the general wave of persecutions by al-Nasir Muhammad.

At the same time, there was also unrest and agitation specific to the region of the Fayyum. Thus we read of tumult and outbreaks of violence against the people of the Fayyum from Yuhanna ibn Wahib during the patriarchate of Cyril III (1235–43). Worse still, in 1302, were the invasions by the Badawi tribes in Upper Egypt and the Baktash in the Fayyum. Stanley Lane-Poole wrote: "The country-side became the scene of horrible massacres, and the corpses poisoned the air." The Christians were to adopt again the blue turbans and the Jews the yellow, and neither were permitted to ride horse or mule.

According to our present state of information, two possible dates for the massacre of Naqlun have been advanced: the last years of the eighteenth century and the beginning of the fourteenth century. Whereas Professor Godlewski considers the victims of the massacre to be secular persons, Anba Abra'am of the Fayyum and the monks of the Monastery of Saint Gabriel view them as martyrs for the Christian faith.

Saints Bane, Simeon, Bashnuna, and Julius of Aqfahs

Coptic hagiology is now experiencing an unprecedented revival. Several contemporary factors have contributed to this awareness and appreciation of the Coptic hagiological heritage. First, since the mid-twentieth century, the general renaissance of the church has produced an indigenous historical scholarship concerned with the study of the roots of the Coptic faith and its traditions. Secondly, the numerous translations of Coptic relics from the West to Egypt have indirectly promoted the study of saints. Thirdly, the discoveries of holy relics and their translation from one site to another have done their part in producing a collective consciousness of the significance and importance of the *ecclesia triumphans*. The various neo-Coptic schools of Christian art have specialized in portraying the 'athletes of God' and the treasures of Coptic Church history in their typically Egyptian environment. These factors, as well as the deliberate promotion of the glories of the past, have been instrumental in the determined search for and study of the confessors and martyrs of the Coptic Church.

The general trend to accept and value the piety, faith, and asceticism of certain 'holy men' has been a typical characteristic of many modern Copts. In light of this observation, there are numerous new 'saints' whose reputation for holiness has been well attested.

Apa Bane

The discovery of the mummy of the fourth-century Apa Bane (Abu Fana) in 1992 by the international archaeological team under Professor Helmut Buschhausen of Vienna represents the most significant find in the realm of Coptic hagiology. The saint was embalmed and bandaged in precious linen and rested on a layer of incense in a shaft tomb. Since 1987 Buschhausen's team of archaeologists representing seven European universities has been excavating the site of Dair Abu Fana, thirty kilometers south of Minya at the edge of the desert near Qasr Hor. While the vita of this famous Upper Egyptian saint was known, only the recent paleopathological examinations and analyses of the skeletal structure could confirm some of the strange ascetic practices of Apa Bane.

Both the Sa'idic version of the *Apophthegmata Patrum* (fifth/sixth century) and the fifth-century *Historia Monachorum in Aegypto* provide information about this saint. He left his native village of Abusir near Hermopolis Magna (al-Ashmunain) to live for eighteen years in the absolute darkness of a cave. He never lay down to rest; even while eating and sleeping, he stood up, resting his body against a wall. This practice led to a kind of humpback that people compared with the bending of a palm—*Bane* in the Upper Egyptian dialect means 'palm.' The soles of his feet were described as being like leather and those of an elephant. He was known to be able to fast for thirty-seven days, three days less than the fast of Christ. People entrusted him with their money, which he distributed to the needy. Apa Bane also predicted the death of the emperor Theodosius I in 395.

The examination of his skeleton revealed that Apa Bane may have lived for forty years. Already by the age of twenty-two, he may have suffered from inflammation and fusing of the vertebrae. Apa Bane may have been born around 355 and died shortly after the death of the emperor Theodosius in 395.

After his death, a large monastic community emerged. The memorial Church of Apa Bane (late fifth century) may have been in many ways comparable to the Church of the Metamorphosis at Saint Catherine's in the Sinai. In the twelfth and thirteenth centuries, the monastery must have enjoyed some prestige. At this time the church was adorned with frescoes. Moreover, Theodosius II (1294–1300), the seventy-ninth successor to the throne of

Saint Mark, had once served as a monk at Dair Abu Fana. The fifteenth-century historian al-Maqrizi described the Monastery of Bu Fana: "It is built of stone and of fine architecture. It belongs to the district of al-Minya, and formerly there were a thousand monks here, but now only two; it lies on the dam below the mountain." The site was rediscovered in 1706 by the Jesuit father Claude Sicard.

On Amshir 25 (March 4), 1992, the Copts in the diocese of Mallawi gathered for a service in the memorial church. However, in 1993 the church was seriously damaged in an earthquake. Two years later, the church was desecrated and the liturgical vessels were stolen. Bishop Demetrius ordered an icon painted of Apa Bane, which shows the stiff and bent posture of the saint.

Saint Simeon, the Pious Tanner

From 1989 to 1991, Coptic clergymen and archaeologists searched for the relics of the tenth-century tanner Simeon. According to the medieval Coptic synaxaria, he was buried in the cemetery of al-Habash in Old Cairo. The synaxarion for Abib 19 (July 26) commemorates the life and death of Pope John X (1363–69), who was buried next to Simeon the Tanner. The same source also refers to the ministry and death of Pope Gabriel IV (1370–78), who died on Bashans 3 (May 11) and was also buried next to Simeon.

In the course of the restorations of the ancient Church of the Holy Virgin in Babylon al-Darag in Old Cairo, the relics of the saint were discovered on Sunday, August 4, 1991. They rested about one meter below the surface of the church. The official text announcing the discovery reads:

> The skeleton belongs to a person who died in his late forties, or in his early fifties. He is short of stature, small in size, of brilliant and beautiful features. The miraculous wonder is that the hair of his head remained intact and did not disintegrate because of the high humidity of the place. This indicated that this person had a bald head in the front, but had very thick hair in the back of his head that reached down to the back of his neck.

Indeed, a nineteenth-century icon of the pope Abraham ibn Za'ra (975–78) in the Church of the Holy Virgin al-Mu'allaqa also includes the bald-headed tanner carrying two water jars. This painting depicts some of the characteristics of the discovered skeleton.

Moreover, outside the nearby Church of Saints Cyrus and John (south of Qasr al-Sham'), a clay pot more than one thousand years old was discovered. It is believed that this was the vessel that Simeon used to provide water to the destitute. This jar is now képt in the new Church of Saint Simeon on Muqattam, Cairo.

In view of the discovery of the relics of this saint, Pope Shenuda III ordered that "the relics should be divided between three churches only, namely the Church of the Holy Virgin in Babylon al-Darag, the Church of the Holy Virgin al-Mu'allaqa, and the Church of Saint Simeon the Tanner, Muqattam, Cairo." On July 9, 1992, Anba Mattawus, general bishop for Old Cairo, deposited relics of the saint in the Church in Babylon al-Darag. Two days later they were presented to the Church of Saint Simeon.

The significance of the faith of the tanner Simeon lies in his trust in the omnipotence of God, by which even the mountain could be moved to the Muqattam. During the reign of the caliph al-Mu'izz (972–75), a certain Jew named Moses disputed with the patriarch Abraham in the presence of the caliph about the truth of the gospel. He asked him about the following statement: "If ye have faith as a grain of mustard-seed, ye shall say unto this mountain: 'Remove hence to yonder place; and it shall remove . . . .'" (Matt. 17:20). Thereupon the caliph asked the patriarch, "What sayest thou concerning this word? Is it in your gospel or not?" Anba Abraham answered, "Yes, it is in it." The caliph demanded this miracle be performed by Abraham's hands, otherwise he would destroy the patriarch with his sword. Anba Abraham requested three days to beseech the Lord. He brought together the monks, priests, elders, and all the Orthodox people and imposed on them a penance to stay for three days in the church.

In the morning of the third day, while praying in the Church of the Holy Virgin al-Mu'allaqa, the patriarch saw the Holy Virgin, who advised him to proceed to the great market. "There thou wilt find a one-eyed man carrying on his shoulder a jar full of water; seize him, for he it is at whose hands this miracle shall be manifested." The patriarch followed the advice of the Holy Virgin, and he met the man, a tanner, who had plucked out his eye on account of the commandment of the Lord (Matt 5:29) and carried water to the poor people who had no money to buy it from the water-carrier.

The tanner told the patriarch, "Go out with thy priests and all thy people to the mountain in the presence of the caliph and all his soldiers. Then cry aloud, 'O Lord, have mercy' three times, and each time thou shalt prostrate thyself and make the sign of the cross over the mountain." The patriarch followed the words of the tanner, and the mountain was lifted from the ground . . . and came down again. The caliph said, "O patriarch, I have recognized the correctness of thy faith . . . ." (*History of the Patriarchs of the Egyptian Church*, Vol. II, Part ii, Cairo 1948, the Biography of Abraham the Syrian, 135–145).

Apa Bashnuna the New Martyr

In 1991, in the course of some major repairs to the ancient Church of Saints Sergius and Bacchus in Old Cairo—executed by Abuna Ghubriyal Girgis, the parish priest, under the supervision of the Egyptian Antiquities Organization—an important discovery was made. As the workmen dug around the northeastern column of the nave and the northern base of the ambon, they discovered several bones, which, according to Bishop Mattawus, were "surrounded by bricks to form a sort of wall to shield the bones from damage. It was God's infinite care that protected the bones from putrefaction due to the excessive underground waters. The relics were removed with special care on April 25, 1991, Baramuda 17, 1707." Apparently, there was no doubt that the relics belonged to a Copt, since "there was no historical mention of any other saint or person in the Church of Saint Sergius other than Saint Bashnuna, which convinced us that these relics belonged to him."

According to the testimony of medieval visitors, occidental pilgrims were also buried in the church. Sultan al-Nasir Muhammad (1310–14) had transferred to the Franciscans certain rights and privileges in this church, which they retained for several centuries. Greffin Affagart (1533/34), in his *Relation de Terre Sainte* (Paris, 1902, 68), refers to "le bon seigneur de la Rivière" who was buried in this church. Brocardi mentioned in a letter dated October 16, 1556, that in this church is the tomb of the Venetian merchant Alfonso Basalu (Monneret de Villard, "Ricerche," BSRGE XII, 1923, 225) and Paul Lucas knew "that many Franks had been buried there" (*Voyage* I, 1704, 225).

The Coptic historical sources provided Anba Mattawus, the general bishop for Old Cairo, and Abuna Ghubriyal Girgis with a clue to the identity of the bodily remains. The vita of Pope John V (1147–66) in the *History of the Patriarchs of the Egyptian Church* relates that during the caliphate of al-'Adid (1160–71), the Turkoman al-Ghuzz killed the wazir Dirgham and chaos reigned in Cairo. The thirteenth-century Coptic synaxarion confirms this report, namely that "on Bashans 24 [June 1]—on the day when the Lord Jesus Christ and His family entered Egypt . . . and when on their return they stopped in the cave of the Church of St. Sergius and Bacchus in Old Cairo— the holy Bashnuna suffered martyrdom. This was in A.M. 880, or A.D. 1164. The faithful came and gathered the remains of the body of Saint Bashnuna, and they transferred them to the Church of St. Sergius and Bacchus in Old Cairo, where they buried him."

Following their discovery in April 1991, the relics were placed in a specially manufactured wooden tube. Some of the relics were given to the late Abuna 'Abd al-Masih Girgis, parish priest of the Church of Saint Menas in Fumm al-Khalig. He placed them in a special wooden tube and anointed them with scents and perfumes. Since then, several miracles of healing through the intercession of Saint Bashnuna have been reported.

Julius of Aqfahs, Biographer and Writer

In 1994, during the restoration of the Church of Saint Shenuda in Dair Abu al-Saifain in Old Cairo, workmen discovered several bones of nameless persons beneath the floor of the narthex between the two Roman columns. A Coptic monk of the Monastery of Abu Mina in Maryut is said to have experienced a vision of the saint, thereby identifying the bones as those belonging to Saint Julius of Aqfahs. It is a noteworthy coincidence that in 1993, the Coptic scholar Yuhanna Nessim Yussef submitted his doctoral dissertation, *Recherches sur Jules d'Akfahs,* to the University of Montpellier in France. Though this study mentions the funerary stele of the saint, it makes no reference to his relics. A copy of the well-known icon of Saint Julius by Ibrahim al-Nasikh (A.M. 1471/A.D. 1755), in the Church of Saint Mercurius was made on July 14, 1995, and adorns the shrine of Saint Julius in the narthex of the Church of Saint Shenuda—next to the recently discovered relics of the Akhmim martyrs and Saints Dioscorus and Aesculapius. Saint Julius served as a Roman officer who was sympathetic to the martyrs of the Diocletian persecutions. He is credited with preserving many relics and composing a special cycle of the martyrdoms he witnessed. Toward the end of the persecutions, he sought martyrdom and made a public confession of faith. The governor of Samannud executed him. Over 1,500 witnesses were converted by his pious sacrifice.

The Veneration of Saints

THE earliest recorded reference to the veneration of the relics of a saint is found in the description of the martyrdom of Saint Polycarp of Smyrna in the middle of the second century. Following his death, the Christians tried to obtain his corpse, since, as Eusebius Pamphilus relates, "many of us eagerly wished to have communion with the sacred body . . . . At last we took his bones, more valuable than precious stones, and more tried than gold, we deposited them where it was proper they should be" (*The Ecclesiastical History* IV, 15).

Another early tradition of veneration involved the head of Mark the Evangelist. Coptic tradition mentions that in 646 the patriarch Benjamin I "carried the head in his bosom and the priests went before him . . . then he made a chest of plane wood with a padlock upon it, and placed the head therein" (*History of the Patriarchs of the Coptic Church*, Patrologia Orientalis, vol I, 494–500). The origin of this story should be assigned to the twelfth century, the time when the head of Mark played a central role in the service of consecration of Coptic popes. At the time of the pontificate of Christodoulus (1047–77), the head of the evangelist reposed in a chest in the house of Abu Yahya Sakarya, later in the home of Gabriel ibn Quzman. From there, the chest was taken to the residence of Mansur ibn Mufarrig in Alexandria. Toward the thirteenth century, we lose track of the chest with the relics.

Today, the oldest Coptic reliquary is in the museum of the Monastery of the Syrians in Wadi al-Natrun. This ebony chest, which measures 149 by 49 by 34 centimeters, was discovered in the keep (*qasr*) of the monastery by H. Hauser in 1909. The chest is entirely plain except for the front, which is enriched with intarsia. The lid, which is of a later date than the body, is constructed of pine with an inserted axial band of carved panels. In style and design, the lid shows similarities to the sanctuary door of the Church of Saint Macarius in the Monastery of Saint Macarius (twelfth–thirteenth century). The ivory representations on the front of the reliquary show, from left to

right: Michael, James, John the Baptist, Christ as Emmanuel, the Holy
Virgin, Saint Theodore, and Saint Eustathius. Except for the lid, the chest is
contemporary with the altar screen of the Church of the Holy Virgin in the
Monastery of the Holy Virgin, Dair al-Surian, and, therefore, should be
assigned to the first third of the tenth century. According to a list in MS 76
of the Monastery of the Syrians—a commentary on the Gospel of Matthew
by Saint John Chrysostom—this feretory contained the relics of Saints
Severus, Dioscorus, Cyriacus and his mother Julietta, Theodore the Oriental,
James the Sawn-Asunder, John Colobus, Moses the Black, and the Forty
Martyrs of Sebaste, as well as some hair of Mary Magdalene. This feretory is
the sole survivor of the earliest type of Coptic reliquary.

The use of chests for keeping relics seems to have been quite common
among the Copts. Abu al-Makarim mentions that "the body of the great saint
Shenuda the Archimandrite is in a monastery at the top of the mountain
called Athribah; it was contained in a chest until the invasion of Egypt by
Shirkuh and the Ghuzz, who accompanied him, and who broke open the
chest, and the body was taken out . . . ."

The tradition of relic chests continues today. Following the discovery of
the relics of John the Baptist and the ninth-century-B.C. prophet Elisha in
Lent 1976 in the Church of Saint Macarius in the Monastery of Saint
Macarius, a beautifully decorated chest with cross-intarsia was built. The
carvings on the front panels show the head of John the Baptist and biblical
scenes. The lid of the chest can be used as an antimension (altar table).

Since the seventh century, the Copts have lived in an Islamic society.
Their cult of relics, therefore, has had to appear considerably more modest
than the golden and profusely decorated reliquaries in medieval Western
churches. Moreover, the Copts were not permitted to embellish their churches with precious metals; as a result, they were dependent on wood with inlaid
ivory or bones. For the veneration of their relics, they developed cylinder-like
wooden tubes that they covered with precious silk and velvet. In the monasteries these were kept in shrines and could be moved from the summer to the
winter sanctuary. On special days they could be carried in procession. For the
believers, the relics demonstrated the unity of the *ecclesia triumphans*
(Christians who had entered the life eternal) with the *ecclesia militans*
(Christians who were still fighting the daily battle for righteousness and
grace).

Today, relics of saints can be found in nearly every Coptic church. In
most cases, they are small pieces of a bone or a piece of textile or the like; in
the Church of the Holy Virgin in Harat al-Rum, the Copts possess what is
alleged to be the right hand of Saint Marina.

The Coptic cult of the *corpus incorruptum*, or the belief that a saint's body will not decay, is of relatively recent origin and may have been adopted from Western or Byzantine churches. Whereas in the West, Saint Gregory of Tours mentioned "incorruptibe bodies" as early as the sixth century, this phenomenon appeared rather late among the Copts. When the French naval officer C. S. Sonnini passed the Monastery of Saint Bishoi in January 1778, the monks importuned him to visit their church "for they possessed the body of a saint [Saint Bishoi], which was as fresh and florid as if still alive." The monks still refer to Saint Bishoi as "incorruptible."

To demonstrate for pilgrims the incorruptibility of some of their saints, the Copts have introduced glass sarcophagi. In the Church of the Holy Virgin in Damietta, a new glass sarcophagus for the incorruptible body of the nineteenth century Saint Sidhom Bishoi (Baramhat 17/March 26) has been placed in the basement of the church. Also, the relics of the incorruptible Saint Yusab ibn al-Abahh, metropolitan of Girga and Akhmim from 1735 to 1826 (Tuba 17/January 25), repose in a glass sarcophagus in the Church of the Holy Apostles in the Monastery of Saint Antony.

New tube-sarcophagi for the 'classical desert fathers' whose relics repose as *corpus totum* have been installed for Saints Bishoi and Paul of Tammua in the Monastery of Saint Bishoi, Saint John Kame in the Monastery of the Syrians, and Saints Moses the Black and Isidore in the Monastery of al-Baramus.

The festive translation of relics from one place to another is also a relatively new practice among the Copts, although an example was set by the monks of the Monastery of Saint Macarius. In the eighth century, they stole the relics of Saint John Colobus, which reposed in the Melkite Monastery of Saint Antony at the Red Sea, and deposited them in the Monastery of Saint Macarius, Wadi al-Natrun. In the fourteenth century, the relics of Saint Menas were transferred from his shrine in the desert of Mareotis to the Church of Saint Menas at Fumm al-Khalig, Cairo. The relics of the popular Bishop Abra'am of the Fayyum (1829–1914) were transferred on May 16, 1987, from the Church of Saint Mercurius in Dair al-'Azab, south of Madinat al-Fayyum, to the newly erected pilgrims' center east of the Church of Saint Mercurius. The relics of Saint Mikha'il al-Buhayri (1847–1923) were transferred on February 23, 1991, from his tomb to the choir of the Church of Saint George in Dair al-Muharraq, while other relics of the saint were taken to his native village of Ishnin al-Nasara and to Dair al-'Azab.

The veneration of relics occurs with the annual aromatization of the reliquary on the feast of his martyrdom by the local bishop, or in some cases, by the pope. These aromatic spices are used in the service of the burial of Christ on Good Friday, when the priest spreads over the icon of the Burial of Christ or the Crucifixion roses and the aromatic spices, which are then covered with a veil known as the *prospherein*.

With these powdered aromatic spices, called *hanut,* the reliquary is blessed. Nuns prepare the *hanut* with the following ingredients: *gawz al-tib* (nutmeg), *habbahan* (cardamom), *zirr al-ward* (Indian sphaeranthus), *sunbul* (spikenard), *khuzami* (mignonette), *salikhat* (cassia), *'ud al-salib* (peony), *qirfa* (cinnamon bark), *qurunfil* (clove), *qasab al-dharirat* (myrtle sedge), *murr* (myrrh), and *mai'at* (storax).

The Coptic Pilgrimage

Religious and Profane Aspects

ORIGINALLY, pilgrimage sites were places where God had revealed himself in one way or another. Thus certain sites in the Judeo-Christian tradition of a community were regularly visited in the hopes of acquiring those spiritual benefits that their ancestors had experienced there. Instead of being blessed directly by saints and other unusually gifted persons, later generations had to be satisfied with the veneration of their tombs or their relics. Judging from the graffiti on tomb walls, already by the third century Christians were visiting the tombs of the martyrs in expectation of 'divine happenings,' of healing and other miracles. Pilgrimages were also an occasion for prayer and sincere devotion. In some cases, pilgrimages served as a means of atoning for one's sins, receiving expiation, or attaining a special pardon. To this day, pilgrimages are made as a response, as an act of obedience to a promise or a vow made, as an act of penance.

One of the greatest critics of the popular religion in his day was the outspoken archimandrite Shenuda (333–451) of the White Monastery at Suhag. He was greatly concerned with uprooting the widespread pagan customs in the church. This included magic spells and other forms of heathen practices that had survived from earlier times. Speaking of the pilgrimages to the shrines of the Christian martyrs, his words are worth repeating, since they apply as much to our day:

> To go to the shrine of the martyr, to pray, to read, to sing psalms, to be sanctified, to partake of the Eucharist in the fear of Christ is well and good . . . . But to talk, to eat and to drink, to frolic, or rather, shall I say to fornicate, and to commit murder as a result of drinking and lewdness and brawls, with complete stupidity, that is lawlessness. While some are indoors, singing Psalms, reading, taking communion, others outside fill the place with the din of trumpets and pipes . . . . Ye have made the

house of God a place to sell honey in, and bracelets. Ye have made the shrines into prowling grounds for your cattle, race tracks for your donkeys and your horses . . . . Things that are not even done in the marketplace to vendors have been done to vendors at the shrines of the martyrs . . . . If your daughters and mothers are going to put perfume on their heads and black paint on their eyes and beautify themselves to deceive people who look at them; and your son, your brother, your neighbor does the same when he goes to the place of the martyr, then what are your houses for? There are many who go to the shrines for the purpose of polluting 'the temple of God' and making the 'members of Christ' harlot members, instead of keeping them holy and free from all defilement, whether it be a man or a woman . . . . Do not make visits to the shrines of the martyrs the occasion of destroying your flesh in the tombs round about them, or in the buildings near by, or in the corners inside them . . . .

Many pilgrimages in Egypt last up to seven days, such as those to the Convent of Saint Damiana at Bilqas or the Church of Saint George at Mit Damsis. Other pilgrimages last merely three days, like the one to the Holy Virgin at Daqadus. Most pilgrimages commence on the preceding evening of the feast (the vigil) and conclude after the Divine Liturgy on the following day, as for example at Sibirbai (Tanta) on Ba'una 12 (June 19). The main service normally takes place on the vigil of the feast, generally known as 'the great night.' At this occasion special processions with banners, icons, and relics take place.

Several customs and rites are followed at most Coptic pilgrimages. People attend the feasts to pray, offer gifts and make promises or vows, seek healing from mental and physical ailments, and give donations to the less fortunate. The prayers are generally made in front of the altar, a wonder-working icon, or the relics of the saint. In view of the increased demand by pilgrims to hold and touch relics of saints, there has been in the past ten years an unprecedented supply of relics. For months many pilgrims save their money for the occasion of the pilgrimage. In some cases the offerings take the form of incense, icons, even sanctuary curtains—all articles that the church might need. I have seen farmers offer a young lamb, which is slaughtered in the churchyard. The recipients of the meat are the priests, the poor, and family members.

Following promises they have made, parents bring their children to the feast to have them baptized. At Dair al-Muharraq, often more than one thousand children are baptized during the feast. Following the baptism, the children are marked with red ribbons and the parents take them to receive the Holy Eucharist. In some places, like at Saint Damiana, the godparents will lift the child on a horse or a donkey for a local parade. At some monasteries in Upper Egypt, baptisms are carried out in relays, by vigorous monks and priests, so that each baptism lasts less than ten seconds.

Many Muslims attend the Coptic pilgrimages as well, especially in Upper Egypt. At the Church of the Holy Virgin at Gabal al-Tayr, there is a baptistry filled with unconsecrated water. I was told that it is for Muslims who come here to immerse their children when they are afraid that they might be dying. This imitation of Christian baptism carried out for Muslims was already noted in the thirteenth century by the Hanbalite theologian Ibn Taymiya.

Women who want children, single people who want to get married, sick people looking for healing, students who want to pass their examinations—all of them turn to the saints. In some places, as, for example, at Mit Damsis or Dimuqrat, the monks practice various rites of exorcism, healing those who are believed to be demon-possessed. According to reports of pilgrimages in the fourth and fifth centuries, the churches served as hospitals. There were saints who were called upon for general diseases, ailments, and difficulties and others who were sought after in cases of eye, ear, or throat diseases.

However, just as Shenuda the Archimandrite described, there is also a purely profane side to the Coptic pilgrimage. This has called forth criticism and censure not only in the fifth century but also by the clergy of today. During the days, but also at night, many pilgrims gather in restaurants and coffee- and teashops and visit theatrical shows that are set up in the neighborhood of the churches and monasteries. The villages are illuminated at night with strings of colorful electric lamps. There are stands selling sweetmeats, candy, crystallized honey, sugared almonds, and beet-sugar; the butchers offer sausages and kebab. The grocer sells various spices, pastries, and hummus, which the pilgrims purchase for their families and neighbors. There are always those selling dried fish, which is a specialty at the Coptic pilgrimage. For entertainment, there are scattered around 'dancing horses,' merry-go-rounds, and smaller and larger swings. Shops sell souvenirs, plastic dolls, toys, and music boxes. At another corner is a gambling table. A large assortment of religious souvenirs and mementos are offered, from inexpensive copies of Byzantine icons and plastic statuettes of the Holy Virgin of Zaytun to prints of Guido Reni's *Ecce Homo* and Carlo Dolci's *Mater Dolorosa*. Tapes of Coptic liturgical music and sermons by Pope Shenuda III are constantly played to attract the pilgrims to the booths and stalls. The tattooist offers a large assortment of secular and religious designs; generally, Copts have a cross, the Holy Virgin, or a saint with the date of the pilgrimage tattooed on the inside of the right wrist.

Pilgrimage Sites of Today

With the recent increased mobility of Christians in Egypt and the dynamic developments within the Coptic Church, the popularity of several pilgrimage centers has reflected these rapid changes. Pilgrimage centers are normally endowed with certain 'supernatural qualities,' which respond to spiritual needs. As large sections of the population move from one place to another, some sites are abandoned, while others emerge.

The Monastery of Saint Menas at Maryut, in the Western Desert
The first small oratory in the form of a tetrapylon with the relics of the martyr was built during the papacy of Athanasius I (328–73). At the request of Pope Theophilus, the emperor Arcadius enlarged the building sometime between 395 and 412. The pilgrimage site, on account of its therapeutic waters, achieved its greatest importance in the fifth and sixth centuries, after the great basilica, the largest church in Egypt, was erected in 401. At the beginning of the seventh century, the shrine was in the hands of the Greeks, for we hear of the visit of the Greek Orthodox patriarch Saint John the Almoner to the desert of Mareotis. On account of the Persian invasion of Egypt (619) and the Arab conquest (641), the shrine suffered severely. During the papacy of Michael I (743–67), the Copts acquired the site. In 815 the church was pillaged by the Bedouins, though Pope Joseph (831–49) repaired most of the damage at Saint Menas. In the latter part of the ninth century, the church and monastery were again demolished. In the eleventh century, some monks still lived there, but the church no longer served as a pilgrimage center.

The pilgrimage center was rediscovered in 1905 by Msgr. C. M. Kaufmann. Subsequently the site was excavated by the archaeologists of the Coptic Museum and the German Archaeological Institute in Cairo. On November 27, 1959, Pope Cyril VI laid the foundation stone for the new monastery. Since November 23, 1972, with the deposition of the body of Pope Cyril VI in the crypt under the major altar of the new basilica, this site has become one of the major pilgrimage centers in Lower Egypt, especially on Ba'una 12 (June 19) and Hatur 15 (November 24). Extensive accommodations enable pilgrims to spend several days at the site. Two kiosks with a large assortment of devotional material serve the increasing number of visitors.

The Church of Saint George at Mit Damsis

The village of Mit Damsis, ten kilometers north of Mit Ghamr in the province of Daqahliya, is situated on the Damietta branch of the Nile. The church is in fact composed of two separate buildings enclosed by a wall. The famous relic of Saint George is kept in the old church, which supposedly was built by Queen Helena, the mother of Constantine, in 328. The new church was built in 1880, and the beautiful circular mosaic above the entrance was finished in 1961. Many pilgrims, both Christian and Muslim, who suffer from various ailments spend the nights from Misra 17 to 25 (August 23–31) in the Church of Saint George, expecting to be visited by the saint and be healed. The *mulid* at Mit Damsis is one of the largest pilgrimages in the Delta.

The Church of Saint Rebecca at Sunbat, Daqahliya

Sunbat is a small village on the Damietta branch of the Nile almost opposite Mit Damsis. The major pilgrimage to Sunbat takes place in conjunction with the *mulid* of Saint George at Mit Damsis toward the end of August. Others visit the Church of Saint Rebecca on Tut 7 (September 17). Miracles are expected through the relics of Saint Rebecca and her five children, Agathon, Peter, Amon, John, and Amona, all originally from Qus in Upper Egypt. In addition, the relics of the two martyrs Pirou and Athom of Tasempoti, the Coptic name of Sunbat, are kept here.

The Church of the Holy Virgin at Daqadus

The annual pilgrimage to this church takes place between Misra 14 and 16 (August 20–22). The village is situated on the Damietta branch of the Nile a few kilometers north of Mit Ghamr. The present church was built in the nineteenth century on the foundations of a medieval church that was discovered in 1970. According to tradition, the holy family passed through Daqadus on the way to Samannud. The villagers ascribe miraculous qualities to their icon of the Holy Virgin of Daqadus.

The Church of Saint Mercurius at Zifta

On Hatur 25 (December 4) and Abib 25 (August 1), the dates of the two feasts commemorating Saint Mercurius (Abu al-Saifain), pilgrims assemble at his church in Zifta on the Damietta branch of the Nile facing Mit Ghamr. The medieval church was dedicated to Saint Iskhirun of Qallin, though the altar screen from A.M. 1585 (A.D. 1868/69) carried the name of Saint Apa Nub of Samannud. The present church was built in the twentieth century.

The Church of Apa Nub at Samannud

The feast of Apa Nub takes place on Abib 24 (July 31) and Ba'una 23 (June 30); the latter date draws a larger crowd. Samannud, the ancient Sebennytos or Zeb-nuter, is situated east of Mahalla al-Kubra. It was the home of three Coptic popes: John III (680–89), Menas I (767–76), and Cosmas II (851–58). The twelve-year-old Apa Nub of Nahisa near Talkha in Daqahliya suffered martyrdom during the Diocletian persecution in 304. His relics repose in the Church of Apa Nub in Samannud. According to tradition, the holy family passed through Samannud, and Jesus is said to have blessed the water of the well there. This well is now in the inner court of the church.

The Convent of Saint Damiana

The Convent of Saint Damiana is situated a few kilometers north of the town of Bilqas in the province of Daqahliya. According to Coptic tradition, Saint Damiana and her forty virgins suffered martyrdom in 304. Queen Helena is said to have constructed the first Church of Saint Damiana, which was consecrated by Pope Alexander I (312–28) on Bashans 12 (May 20), 326.

Today there are five holy buildings within the convent compound: the old Church of Saint Damiana, the second, nineteenth-century Church of Saint Damiana and her Forty Virgins, the tomb of Saint Damiana and the virgins (1879), the Church of Saint Antony (1973), and the Church of Saint George of Damira (Ba'una 19/June 26). Special tombs are being constructed for the following bishops: Anba Butrus (1925–30), Anba Timotheos (1930–68), and Anba Andarawus (1968–72). A large pilgrimage takes place between Baramuda 27 and Bashans 12 (May 5–20) and on Tuba 13 (January 21).

On November 18, 1973, Pope Shenuda III inaugurated the Convent of Saint Damiana, which is now occupied by approximately eighty contemplative nuns and thirty consecrated women. One of the new cherished relics is a part of Queen Helena, which was deposited in the altar of the old church.

The Church of the Holy Virgin at Sakha

Sakha, the former Xois, is situated two kilometers south of Kafr al-Shaikh. On account of the visit of the holy family, Sakha has been turned into a major pilgrimage shrine. The chief relic here is a stone, discovered in 1985, that bears the footprint of the Christ child and has engraved on its side the word 'Allah.' Pilgrims come to anoint the stone, and traces of the oil are visible on it. The church also holds the relics of Saint Severus, the patriarch of Antioch (d. 538); Zechariah, the eighth-century bishop of Sakha; and Saint Agathon the Stylite, who lived one hundred years: forty in the world, ten in the desert of Scetis, and fifty seated on a column. The present church was rebuilt with permission from Muhammad Ali.

The Church of Saint George at Birma

On Ba'una 3 (June 10), Copts and Muslims take part in the annual Saint George pilgrimage and procession in Birma, eleven kilometers northwest of Tanta. According to the Coptic synaxarion, the Church of Saint George in Birma was the first church in Egypt dedicated to this equestrian warrior-saint. His relics reposed in Birma and were transferred at the end of the four-teenth century to the Monastery of Saint Samuel in the desert of Qalamun on Abib 16 (July 23). The present church was built in 1611, but recently renovated. On January 1, 2000, the Holy Virgin is said to have appeared in the church. A visible mark of the apparition of the Holy Virgin has remained on one of the columns in the nave.

The Church of Saint George at Mahalla Markum

In the small village of Mahalla Markum, six kilometers northwest of Tanta, the Copts of the neighborhood join in the annual July pilgrimage to the modern Church of Saint George (1860), which was built on the site of an older church from the fifteenth century. The original church was built to hold the relics of Saint George, which are venerated in the village.

The Church of Saint Michael at Sibirbai

On Ba'una 12 (June 19) a pilgrimage takes place to the Church of the Archangel Saint Michael in the village of Sibirbai, five kilometers northeast of Tanta. At one time, the village of Sibirbai belonged to the archdiocese of Jerusalem.

The Church of Saint George at Tukh al-Nasara

The pilgrimage Church of Saint George at Tukh al-Nasara, known today as Tukh Dalaka, in the province of Minufiya, is situated about six kilometers north of al-Shuhada'. The annual fair in honor of the saint takes place Baramuda 19 through 26 (April 27–May 4). The pilgrimage church was built in 1770. In addition, there are two churches dedicated to the Holy Virgin in the village. The 'old church,' said to have been built in the eighth century, was rebuilt in 1872. The other church belongs to the dependency of the Monastery of al-Baramus in Wadi al-Natrun and was consecrated in 1876. Three Coptic popes, Matthew III (1631–46), John XVI (1676–1718), and Cyril VI (1959-71), came from Tukh al-Nasara.

The Church of Saint Sarapamon at al-Batanun

Al-Batanun is a small village ten kilometers northeast of Shibin al-Kom in the province of Minufiya. The pilgrimage takes place on Ba'una 27 and 28 (July 4 and 5) and on Hatur 28 (December 7). The church was dedicated in 1897 to Saint Sarapamon, the fourth-century bishop of Nikiu. Saint Sarapamon, of Jewish descent from Jerusalem, was baptized by Pope Theonas (282–300) and joined the Monastery of the Ennaton. Pope Peter I (d.310) consecrated him bishop of Nikiu, and he suffered martyrdom during the Diocletion persecutions. Pope Shenuda I (859–80) also came from al-Batanun. In addition to those relics in the church in al-Batanun, since 1980 some relics of Saint Sarapamon have been venerated in the new Church of the Holy Virgin Qasriyat al-Rihan in Old Cairo.

The Monastery of Saint Bishoi, Wadi al-Natrun

On November 14, 1971, Pope Shenuda III decided to establish his papal desert residence in the Monastery of Saint Bishoi. Prior to this date, this monastery had existed in the shadow of the neighboring Monastery of the Syrians. But now, many Copts visit the monastery in hopes of getting a glimpse of the pope, who spends the latter part of the week here. Every year since 1972, on Abib 8 (July 15), large numbers of Coptic pilgrims have visited the Church of Saint Bishoi to venerate the relics of Saints Bishoi and Paul of Tammua. The relics of Saint Bishoi are believed to be incorruptible.

The Church of the Holy Virgin at Musturud

According to Coptic tradition, the holy family rested on their flight to Egypt in Musturud, where the Christ child blessed the water of the well. The town of Musturud is situated north of Cairo on the banks of the Ismailia Canal. On Ba'una 7 and 8 (June 14 and 15), pilgrims venerate in the old church the miraculous icon of the Holy Virgin, first noted by the Dominican friar Michael Wansleben in 1672. The pilgrims descend to the crypt to drink from the therapeutic water of the well. Many visitors spend the night in the church before they proceed the next morning to the tree of the Holy Virgin in Matariya.

The Tree of the Holy Virgin in Matariya

The northeastern suburb of Cairo has attracted Christian pilgrims ever since the Middle Ages. The tree of Matariya is said to have offered shade to the holy family. Their visit to Matariya is not only well attested by the Gospel of Pseudo-Matthew and the Coptic and Ethiopic synaxaria, but it is also mentioned by medieval pilgrims to the Holy Land. According to the Ethiopic synaxarion, when the holy family approached Matariya, there was a staff in the hand of Joseph wherewith he used to smite Jesus, but Joseph gave this rod to Jesus. Then said Jesus unto his mother: "We will tarry here," and that place and its desert and the well became known as Matariya. And Jesus took Joseph's staff and broke it into little pieces, and planted these pieces in that place, and he dug with his own divine hands a well, and there flowed from it sweet water, which had an exceedingly sweet odor. And Jesus took some of the water in his hands, and watered therewith the pieces of wood which he had planted, and straightaway they took root, and put forth leaves, and an exceedingly sweet perfume was emitted by them. And these pieces of wood grew and increased, and they called them 'balsam.' And Jesus said unto his mother: "O my mother, these balsam which I have planted shall abide here for ever, and from them shall be taken the oil for Christian baptism . . . ."

The Pseudo-Matthew Gospel replaces the balsam with a palm tree, a tradition that is also preserved in the Qur'an. According to the Qur'anic version, the Holy Virgin saw the palm tree and wished to rest under it.

The balsam shrubs have long since disappeared. The sycamore tree that now stands at Matariya was planted in 1672. This venerable tree fell, due to old age, on June 14, 1906, but fortunately a living shoot from it remains to this day.

The tree is significant to other Christians as well. Opposite the garden with the tree of the Virgin, the Jesuits dedicated in 1904 a church to the holy family. Annually on December 8, the Catholics participate in a pilgrimage to both the church and the tree of the Virgin.

The Church of the Holy Virgin at Zaytun

Ever since the apparition of the Holy Virgin on the dome of the Church of the Holy Virgin in Shari' Tumanbey, Zaytun, on April 2, 1968, large numbers of pilgrims visit the church, which was built in 1924. This apparition was officially acknowledged by Pope Cyril VI and the Holy Synod, and an annual feast honoring the apparition was proclaimed in 1969.

The Church of Saint Ruwais (Tegi) in 'Abbasiya

Every year on Baba 21 (October 31), pilgrims gather at the tomb of Saint Ruwais, also known as Tegi and Anba Farig, to commemorate the suffering of this 'fool of God' who died in 1404. The small church in the shadow of the new patriarchal Cathedral of Saint Mark (consecrated on July 26, 1968) was built on the former Coptic cemetery of al-Khandaq.

The Church of the Holy Virgin at al-Azbawiya in Azbakiya

Al-Azbawiya is the Cairo dependency of the Monastery of the Syrians, situated in the immediate proximity of the former Coptic patriarchal cathedral at Shari' al-Murqusiya, which served the Coptic patriarchs from 1800 until June 1968. Al-Azbawiya, built in the nineteenth century, also commemorates a site visited by the holy family, and where Jesus is believed to have blessed the water of the nearby well. The church is famous for its 'ancient' icon of the Holy Virgin (60 by 100 centimeters), which is attributed to Luke.

The Church of the Holy Virgin at Ma'adi

According to Coptic tradition, the holy family embarked from Ma'adi to sail to Upper Egypt. It is generally believed that the site is also where the pharaoh's daughter discovered Moses in the bulrushes (Exod. 2:5). Moreover, it is said that in ancient days this was the place of worship of the Israelites when they were in bondage in Egypt. In the thirteenth century, the Coptic church there was named after 'the pure Lady Mary,' or al-Martuti *(meter Theou)*. On March 12, 1976, a deacon discovered a nineteenth-century Protestant pulpit Bible (a Smith–Van Dyck version of 1865) floating in the Nile near the banks of the church. He recovered the Bible, which was open to the page of the prophecy of Isaiah 19:25: "Blessed be Egypt my people." On June 1, 2000, a great celebration commemorated the second millennium of the visit of the holy family to Egypt. Participating in the festivities were high-ranking officials such as Prime Minister Atef Obeid, Foreign Minister Amr Musa, and other cabinet ministers, as well as the shaikh of al-Azhar Muhammad Sayyid Tantawi, Pope Shenuda III, and Patriarch Stephanus II. These and other dignitaries witnessed a laser show and the performance of an eleven-act opera describing the journey of the holy family in Egypt, written by Muhammad Salmawi and directed by Mohammed Nouh.

The Church of Saints Cosmas and Damian at Manyal Shiha

From Ba'una 20 to 22 (June 27–29), pilgrims, especially those suffering from nervous disorders and epilepsy, gather in the Church of Saints Cosmas and Damian in the village of Manyal Shiha between Giza and al-Badrashayn on the west bank of the Nile. The relics of the two 'silverless' physicians repose in a new reliquary on the south wall of the nave. On the west wall of the nave is a new (1985) shrine with an icon of Saint Mohrail and her little brother Hor. They suffered martydrom in 304 and are commemorated on Tuba 14 (January 22).

The Church of Saint Barsum the Naked at Ma'sara

Toward the end of September, many pilgrims from Cairo, Halwan, and Ma'sara gather at the pilgrimage church dedicated to Saint Barsum the Naked. During the Middle Ages this monastery produced two Coptic patriarchs, John VIII (1300–20) and Mark IV (1348–63). For many years, Saint Barsum lived as a hermit in the crypt of the Church of Saint Mercurius in Old Cairo. On account of his witness for Christ, he was arrested and sent to the Monastery of Shahran at Ma'sara. He died in 1318.

The Monastery of the Archangel Gabriel at Naqlun

The Monastery of the Archangel Gabriel is one of the oldest monasteries in the Fayyum. It is situated thirteen kilometers south of Madinat al-Fayyum. Until the middle of the twentieth century, the monastery was abandoned except for the annual pilgrimage, which occurred on Baramuda 22 (April 30), the feast of Saint Isaac al-Hurini. Ever since the discovery of the twelve 'Fayyum martyrs' in August 1991, about 150 meters southwest of the monastic buildings, many Copts from Cairo, the Fayyum, and the Nile Valley visit the monastery. Pilgrimage facilities enable visitors to spend some time at the monastery.

The Monastery of Saint George at Sidmant al-Gabal

Annually at Ascension time, large numbers of pilgrims from Madinat al-Fayyum and the Nile Valley north of Beni Suef assemble at this monastery dedicated to Saint George. Situated on the banks of the Bahr Yusuf Canal, the monastery has extensive facilities that enable visitors to spend several days at Sidmant.

The Church of the Holy Virgin at Bayad al-Nasara

On the east bank of the Nile almost opposite Beni Suef, the Church of the Holy Virgin serves as a pilgrimage center and retreat house for the Coptic Order of the Daughters of Saint Mary, established by the metropolitan Athanasius in 1965. The pilgrimage takes place Misra 1–16 (August 7–22).

The Church of Saint George at Biba

A week prior to the feast of the Ascension, pilgrims gather in the Church of Saint George in Biba, twenty-two kilometers south of Beni Suef. Many visitors suffer from nervous disorders and attend the celebrations in hope of recovery.

The Church of the Holy Virgin at Dair al-Garnus

On Bashans 24 (June 1), pilgrims arrive at the Church of the Holy Virgin seven kilometers west of Ishnin al-Nasara to celebrate the holy family's visit to this village. Here Jesus is believed to have blessed the water of the well. In the fifteenth century, al-Maqrizi mentioned a "monastery of Jesus (Arjanus), where a festival is held on Bashans 25. On the night of this day, a spring bearing the name of Jesus' spring is closed; and in the sixth hour people collect and take away the stone from the well and find that the water within it had risen . . . . From this they reckon how high the Nile will be that year . . . ." Capitals and columns testify to the presence of a sixth-century church.

The Church of the Holy Virgin at al-Garnus

This church in al-Garnus is situated about three kilometers south of Dair al-Garnus, where pilgrims gather for the feast of the Assumption of the Holy Virgin in August. During these days, so the villagers believe, pilgrims are never bitten by vermin, and the children even play with scorpions, as written in Luke (10:19).

The Church of Saint Theodore at Dair al-Sanquriya

The Church of Saint Theodore is situated eighteen kilometers west of Bani Mazar on the eastern bank of the Bahr Yusuf Canal in the region of al-Bahnasa, the former Oxyrhynchus. According to the fourth-century *Historia Monachorum,* about thirty thousand monks and nuns used to live in this region. The present church belongs to the late eighteenth or early nineteenth century. Pilgrims assemble at the church on Abib 20 (July 27) on the feast of Saint Theodore and on Hatur 5 (November 14), commemorating the translation of the relics of Saint Theodore to Shutb, south of Asyut.

The Church of the Holy Virgin at Gabal al-Tayr

Two major Upper Egyptian pilgrimages take place at Gabal al-Tayr ('mountain of the birds') on the east bank of the Nile opposite the village of al-Bayahu, on Tuba 21 (January 29) and Misra 16 (August 22). Supposedly the church was built by Queen Helena in 328, and was restored in 1938 by Bishop Severus of Minya.

The church is carved into the mountainside, and is often called the 'Convent of the Pulley,' because this is the method by which it used to be reached. According to Abu al-Makarim, "in the rock is the mark of the palm of the hand of the Lord Christ which was made when he touched the mountain . . . . He grasped the mountain, when it worshiped before him, and restored it to its place with his hand, so that the mark of his palm remains impressed upon the mountain." This rock with the imprint of the hand of Jesus was removed by Almeric, king of Jerusalem (1162–73) in 1168 and taken to Syria. The church attracts tens of thousands of pilgrims who come from Minya, Asyut, and even Cairo for the feast of the Assumption of the Holy Virgin on Misra 16 (August 22).

The Church of Saint Iskhirun of Qallin at al-Bayahu

The Church of Saint Iskhirun is situated in the southern part of the village of al-Bayahu on the west bank of the Nile between Samalut and Itsa, almost opposite Gabal al-Tayr. The pilgrims gather at the church on Ba'una 7 (June 14) and Baramhat 10 (March 19) and on the feast of the Ascension. Saint Iskhirun refused to sacrifice to the pagan gods and suffered extreme torture and martyrdom during the Decian persecution (249–51).

The Church of Apa Hor at Sawada

Known also as Dair al-Sawada, the church is situated on the east bank of the Nile at the foot of the mountain range four kilometers south of Minya. On Abib 12 (July 19), pilgrims assemble at the subterranean church to commemorate the martyrdom of Apa Hor at Saryaqus near Shibin al-Qanatir. Ancient columns and capitals in the village testify to a former Roman temple, which was later converted into a church. Al-Maqrizi mentioned that the church was destroyed by the Arabs.

The Monastery of the Holy Virgin al-Muharraq at al-Qusiya

Situated west of the village of al-Qusiya on the edge of the desert, the Monastery of the Holy Virgin, known as Dair al-Muharraq, commemorates the final stop of the holy family on their flight to Egypt. Here, at Qusqam, they stayed for six months and some days while Joseph built the first church in Egypt. In the fifth century, at the time of Theophilus and Cyril I (412–44), the church to the Holy Virgin was dedicated and an annual pilgrimage on Hatur 6 (November 15) was instituted. According to the vision of Pope Theophilus (384–412), the risen Lord Jesus together with the apostles, the Holy Virgin, Mary Magdalene, Salome, and Anna traveled on a cloud from Jerusalem to Qusqam, where Peter celebrated the first Eucharist before they all retrurned on a cloud to Jerusalem. During the week of Ba'una 14–21 (June 21–28), more than fifty thousand pilgrims attend the festivities to commemorate the consecration of the first Church of the Holy Virgin at Philippi (al-Qusiya). Until recently, this used to be the largest Christian pilgrimage in Upper Egypt.

The Church of Saint Menas at Dair Shaqlaqil

On the east bank of the Nile and partly built into the mountain opposite the village of Umm al-Qusur (between al-Qusiya and Manfalut) is a church dedicated to Saint Menas. Despite the difficulty of reaching the site, pilgrims gather at this site on Ba'una 15 (June 22) to honor the saint.

The Church of Saint Victor at Shu

The Church of Saint Victor at Shu is situated on the edge of the desert between Abnub and Dair al-Gabrawi on the east bank of the Nile. The annual pilgrimage takes place on Bashans 8 (May 16). On Bashans 9 (May 17), the Coptic Church commemorates Pope Gabriel VIII (1587–1603), who issued liberal laws pertaining to the practices of fasting. (Following his death these laws were revoked.) In a document signed at this church, Gabriel VIII recognized the supremacy of the pope of Rome, in response to the request of Pope Sixtus V (1585–90).

The Monastery of the Holy Virgin at Dair Durunka

About one kilometer southwest of Asyut, on the shelf of the cliff of Istabl 'Antar, is the Monastery of the Holy Virgin, with numerous pilgrimage accommodations built in 1955. More than one hundred thousand pilgrims attend the pilgrimage commemorating the visit of the holy family in Asyut on Misra 1–16 (August 7–22), a pilgrimage that has been occurring since 1960. Since 1990 several apparitions of the Holy Virgin have added to the popular attraction of this monastery, which is administered by the metropolitan of Asyut.

The Coptic Catholics have built a large church at the foot of the mountain. The Coptic Catholics are those Copts who have united with the Roman Catholic Church. Their present patriach is Stephanus II. They number about 300,000 in Egypt.

The Church of Saint George at al-'Awana

On Hatur 7 (November 16), pilgrims gather at the Church of Saint George at al-'Awana to commemorate the miracles of the equestrian saint. The village is situated on the east bank of the Nile north of Abu Tig.

The Church of Saint Bishoi at Sidfa

On Abib 8 (July 15), pilgrims visit the Church of Saint Bishoi at Sidfa, south of Abu Tig. According to a local tradition, Saint Bishoi is believed to be the uncle of Saint Shenuda the Archimandrite. (Actually, Saint Bigoul was the uncle of Saint Shenuda.) Pope John XIII (1484–1524) came from Sidfa.

The Church of the Holy Virgin at Dair al-Ganadla

On the day of the feast of the consecration of the first Church of the Holy Virgin at Philippi on Ba'una 21 (June 28), pilgrims gather at Dair al-Ganadla on the edge of the desert west of Sidfa. Saint Macrobius is commemorated here, as well as at Dair Abu Maqrufa, two kilometers north. Pope Shenuda III has established a center for spiritual retreat at Dair al-Ganadla.

The Monastery of Saint Shenuda the Archimandrite at Suhag

On Abib 7 (July 14), large numbers of pilgrims from Suhag and Akhmim gather at the late-fourth-century Monastery of Saint Shenuda west of Suhag. Since 1975 the monastery has been reoccupied by Coptic monks, and on June 14, 1997, the Holy Synod of the Coptic Church officially recognized this monastery.

The Monastery of Saint Michael at al-Salamuni

The Monastery of the Archangel is situated on the edge of the desert east of al-Salamuni north of Akhmim on the east bank of the Nile. It is the northernmost in the chain of monasteries east of al-Hawawish. Special services for pilgrims are celebrated on Hatur 12 (November 21) and Ba'una 12 (June 19).

The Monastery of the Martyrs at al-Hawawish

This monastery is situated on a slight elevation east of al-Hawawish. A large necropolis extends on both sides of the monastery, which is dedicated to the 8,140 martyrs of Akhmim. Special services for pilgrims are conducted on Tuba 1 (January 9) and Abib 2 (July 9).

The Monastery of Saint George at Dair al-Hadid

The village of Dair al-Hadid is on the east bank of the Nile, eight kilometers south of Akhmim. The monastery was restored in 1870. On Hatur 7 (November 16) and at the time of the Ascension, many Copts attend services at this church. They also visit the monastery on Kiyahk 16 (December 25), the feast of the martyrs Ananias and Khouzi of Akhmim.

The Monastery of Saint Bisada at al-Ahaiwa Sharq

This monastery is on the east bank of the Nile in the village of al-Ahaiwa Sharq, almost opposite al-Manshah, the ancient Ptolemais Hermiou, eighteen kilometers south of Suhag. Saint Bisada suffered martyrdom during the Diocletian persecutions. His relics repose in this monastery. Pilgrimages to this site take place on Kiyahk 27 (January 5), Tuba 24 (February 1), and Abib 27 (August 3), when the faithful venerate their local saint.

The Monastery of Saint Palemon at Qasr al-Sayyad

Annually on Tuba 30 (February 7) and Abib 25 (August 1), pilgrims assemble at the monastery to venerate Saint Palemon, one of the founders of cenobitic monasticism. Saint Pachomius established his first monastery in Tabennesi near the Monastery of Saint Palemon at Chenoboskion, the ancient Qasr al-Sayyad.

The Monastery of Saint Mercurius at Higaza

This monastery is situated in the eastern part of the village of Higaza on the eastern edge of the desert southwest of Qus, between Qina and Luxor. According to tradition, this monastery was established by Queen Helena. In 1911, the church was restored. The pilgrimage commemorating the consecration of the Church of Saint Mercurius takes place on Abib 25 (August 1).

The Convent of Saint Theodore the Warrior at Madinat Habu

This active convent is situated on the west bank of the Nile in the desert about five hundred meters southwest of the temple of Ramses III at Madinat Habu. In the inner court of the convent is also the tomb of the famous Egyptologist Labib Habashi (1905–84). The pilgrims of the region of Luxor venerate Saint Theodore on Abib 20 (July 27).

The Monastery of Saint George at al-Rizaiqat

The largest pilgrimage in Upper Egypt takes place from Hatur 1 to 7 (November 10–16) in the Monastery of Saint George west of Dimuqrat and southwest of Armant. Tens of thousands of pilgrims, both Muslim and Christian, assemble in and around the monastery to visit the miraculous icon of Saint George and experience its blessings.

The Convent of Saint Ammonius and the 3,600 Martyrs of Esna

The convent is situated six kilometers southwest of Esna on the edge of the desert. According to tradition, this site was established by Saint Ammonius with the help of Queen Helena. The church commemorates the 3,600 martyrs who died during the Decian persecutions between 249 and 251. Pilgrims gather at the convent on Kiyahk 14 (December 23).

The Monastery of Saint Pachomius at Idfu

This monastery, restored and activated by Bishop Hadra of Aswan between 1975 and 1980, is situated at Hagir Idfu, five kilometers west of Idfu on the edge of the desert. A few guest rooms enable pilgrims to spend several days at the monastery. The annual pilgrimage takes place on Bashans 14 (May 22).

Coptic Pilgrimages in the Steps of the Holy Family in Egypt

On Thursday, June 1, 2000, high-ranking Egyptian officials gathered at the Church of the Holy Virgin in Ma'adi to commemorate the second millennium of the coming of the holy family to Egypt. An extraordinary opera consisting of eleven musical themes representing the principal stages of the itinerary of the holy family from al-Farama (Pelusium) to the Upper Egyptian Dair al-Muharraq was presented, with the Nile as background. For all Egyptians, with Muslim statesmen and clerics in attendance, this impressive show about the flight of the holy family reinforced religious foundations for the kind of national unity in which Christians and Muslims can accept each other in the spirit of tolerance.

For the Copts the flight of the holy family to Egypt is the fulfillment of several Biblical prophecies. The arrival of Jesus, Mary, and Joseph coincides with the doom of pharaonic Egypt (Isa. 19:1–25). God is about to descend in wrath upon Egypt, bringing the horrors of civil war and tyranny and the destruction of the Egyptian gods. The prophecy of the "altar to the Lord in the midst of Egypt" may have pointed originally to a Jewish temple at Elephantine. The Copts, however, consider it to be in the old Church of the Holy Virgin in Dair al-Muharraq, forty-eight kilometers north of Asyut. The Copts see their divine election confirmed by the prophecy in which God calls the Egyptians "my people." The prophecy "when Israel was a child, I loved him, and out of Egypt I called my son" (Hos. 11:1) is, of course, a reference to God's deliverance of Israel out of the bondage and slavery of Egypt. Matthew personified the original collective sonship and related it to Jesus Christ (Matt. 2:15). The travels of the holy family on the donkey are seen as fulfillment of the messianic prophecy, "Lo, your king comes to you; triumphant and victorious is he, humble and riding on an ass" (Zech. 9:9). Also, the three-and-a-half-year stay of the holy family in Egypt corresponds to the 1,260 days for which the woman with the crown of stars is to flee into the wilderness, where she has a place prepared by God (Rev. 12:6). Traditionally, the woman is interpreted as the heavenly personification of the church, and John depicts Jerusalem, and, by extension, the church as the heavenly bride of Christ (Rev. 21:2). The Copts identify her with the Holy Virgin Mary in Egypt.

One of the so-called 'official' lists of sites visited by the holy family includes twenty places. The sites in the Delta are Musturud, Daqadus, Bilbais, Samannud, the Convent of Saint Damiana, and Sakha. In Cairo the sites are the tree of the Virgin in Matariya; the churches in Harat Zuwayla, Zaytun, and Old Cairo (Saints Sergius and Bacchus); the Church of the Holy

Virgin in Babylon al-Darag; and Ma'adi. In Upper Egypt, the holy family is said to have visited Ishnin al-Nasara, Dair al-Garnus, al-Bahnasa, Gabal al-Tayr, Dair Abu Hinnis, Dairut, Dair al-Muharraq, and Durunka (Asyut). The medieval Coptic and Ethiopian synaxaria list eight sites, while the church historian Abu al-Makarim mentions thirteen 'stopovers' by the holy family in Egypt. In the eleventh-century *History of the Patriarchs of the Egyptian Church,* ten different places are recorded, while in the Coptic psali only six sites are mentioned.

Various reasons account for these discrepancies. There are the purely non-religious factors, the social and economic considerations that have motivated bishops to extend the travels of the holy family to places in their dioceses. For example, in 1955, Bishop Mikha'il of Asyut, probably on the recommendation of members of the local chamber of commerce, announced that the holy family had continued their travels from Dair al-Muharraq at al-Qusiya sixty-one kilometers south to the caves of Istabl 'Antar (Durunka), south of Asyut. Since then, the participants in the annual pilgrimage to Durunka in August have outnumbered the one hundred thousand pilgrims to Dair al-Muharraq, and have brought considerably more business to the region. In a sense, the Holy Virgin Mary has confirmed the episcopal decision, as she has appeared at least three times in Durunka: on January 22, 1980, to a Coptic deacon; on January 10, 1988, to an Australian visitor; and on August 17, 1990, as a bright shining light in the cave.

Bishop Demetrius of Mallawi included not only Mallawi but also the east-bank villages of Bani Hasan, Shaikh 'Abada with Bir al-Sahaba, and Dair Abu Hinnis with Kom Mariam in the itinerary of the divine visitors. For the metropolitan Bishoi of Damietta and Kafr al-Shaikh, it was obvious that the site of the Convent of Saint Damiana at al-Barari was visited by the holy family on the way to the village of Shagarat al-Tin ('fig tree') near Lake Burullus. He was confirming a late-twentieth-century tradition. About two hundred years ago, the parish priest of the village of al-Qusair, on the east bank of the Nile opposite al-Qusiya, pointed out a cave in which the holy family rested before proceeding to Dair al-Muharraq. However, the site could not successfully compete with the traditions of the more influential monks of the monastery.

Recent archaeological discoveries have been used to add new material to the route of the holy family. On September 27, 1984, near the entrance to the Church of the Holy Virgin in Sakha (Kafr al-Shaikh), workers unearthed an eighty-centimeter-long stone with a small brownish dent in it. This the people identified as the footprint of the child Jesus. Ever since, pilgrims have repaired to Sakha to behold this relic, which is said to possess miraculous powers if touched. In 1991, the archaeologist Dr. Mahmud 'Amr of the University of al-Zaqaziq discovered in the temple of Tell Basta (Bubastis) the well that Jesus is believed to have brought forth, providing the citizens with potable water, which became a source of healing for all, except for those who had rejected him.

The recent tradition of the visit of the holy family to the Monastery of Saint Mercurius (Abu al-Saifain) at Tammua, ten kilometers south of Giza, was inspired by a dream of the saintly Pope Cyril VI (1959–71), in which he saw the holy family on the banks of the Nile at the very site where Joseph, son of Jacob, used to have his palace (Gen. 41). Zaytun is also a recent addition to the itinerary: the spectacular apparition of Mary in the spring of 1968 elevated the Cairene suburb to a 'stopover' of the holy family.

In numerous traditions, Jesus was able to detect underground water. For the Egyptians, the need for potable water was always of utmost importance. Therefore, one of the missions of Christ—who is believed to be the living water (John 4:13–15)—was to provide the Egyptians with springs and wells. In Musturud, as at Tell Basta, Jesus caused a well to appear in the cave that had provided shelter for the holy family. Jesus is said to have blessed wells in Harat Zuwayla, Musturud, and several other places. Often the water in these wells, which now usually have churches built around them, is considered to have healing properties. At Ishnin al-Nasara, the blessed well was also used as a Nilometer. People would measure the amount above the bottom of the well: if the water reached 20 cubits, there would be a great abundance in Egypt; if the water was at 18 or 17 cubits, there would also be abundance; but if it stopped at only 16 cubits, there would be great famine throughout Egypt.

From Shaikh 'Abada, on the west bank of the Nile, the holy family proceeded to the northern part of the mountain range near Antina (Antinoë). There they stopped and suddenly a cloud appeared, which provided shade, and a well sprang up. This Bir al-Sahaba was blessed by Jesus. Today a large Islamic cemetery encloses the well. About eight kilometers south of the village of Meir, the holy family discovered a well that was dried up. However, Jesus stretched forth his finger and blessed it as it filled with water. It was here that Salome bathed Jesus while the Holy Virgin gave him milk.

Wadi al-'Ain leads from the desert strip west of al-Hawawish, west of Akhmim, through the mountainous region to Bir al-'Ain. The Bedouins of this region strongly maintain that the water of Bir al-'Ain was blessed by Jesus when the holy family found refuge in their arid wadi. However, to receive a maximum of blessings, the Bedouins add to the water of the spring a little holy water from the well of Zamzam in Mecca!

Certain trees also had a special attraction for the holy family, since the voice of God could appear in trees (Gen. 21:33). The palm tree in Matariya provided not only shade but also dates. In al-Ashmunain (Hermopolis Magna) was a tree that worshiped the traces of Jesus' footsteps. Eventually, Jesus blessed the tree, which had bowed its head when Jesus approached. In Dairut al-Sharif in Upper Egypt, the villagers show the tree of Mary, which is said to be two thousand years old, since it provided shade for the holy family. Muslims visit the tree on Fridays.

Some extraordinary healing miracles are recorded in the Coptic traditions of the flight of the holy family. When they entered Bilbais, they saw a funeral procession, and Jesus had compassion for the mourners. When he heard that the son of a widow had died, he restored the man to life. Thereupon the widow confessed her faith in Christ as the true God. This tradition is undoubtedly a double to the biblical story of the raising of the son of the widow in Nain (Luke 7:11–17). Copts hold that Jesus raised a person from the dead in al-Ashmunain as well. According to the First Infancy Gospel, the child Jesus healed a bride who was deaf and mute. When she took him into her arms and hugged him, her tongue was immediately loosed, her ears were opened, and her speech and hearing were restored. The biblical tradition that Jesus would heal the mute is mentioned by Luke (11:14) and Matthew (9:32–33). In Dairut al-Sharif, Jesus was called on by Dianos, whose son was possessed by a devil, who fought with Jesus, crying out, "What have I to do with you, Jesus of Nazareth . . . ." Jesus said, "Accursed devil, shut up your mouth and come out of him." And the child was healed and many people believed in Jesus. This Upper Egyptian story clearly mimics the healing of the possessed man in Capernaum, as recorded by Mark (1:23–28) and Luke (4:33–37).

The Chains of Saint George

Ever since the fifth century, Western Christians have venerated the chains of the apostle Peter (Acts 12:1–11) in the Basilica of Saint Peter of the Chains, on the Esquiline in Rome. According to tradition, these chains, which were once owned by the Princess Eudoxia, the daughter of the emperor Theodosius II and Eudokia, were sent from Jerusalem to Rome. Many miracles are attributed to these chains, which are kept in a Renaissance tabernacle in the Church of San Pietro in Vincoli. The feast of Saint Peter's Chains (*Petri ad Vincula*) was introduced by Pope Gregory the Great (590–604) and is celebrated on August 1.

In the Middle East, it is the chains not of Saint Peter but of Saint George that are believed to possess miraculous powers to cure the demon-possessed and paralytics. The New Testament narrative of the Gadarene demoniac "who had often been bound with fetters and chains" (Mark 5:3–4) demonstrates that chains were used to restrain the mentally sick. A parallel story in the Coptic tradition tells of Theophanes (952–56), the sixtieth patriarch of Alexandria, who was so overcome by anger that he took off his vestments and the *skhema* (a four-meter-long plaited leather girdle worn by monks), and an unclean spirit descended upon him and struck him down, so that he was bound with iron chains for the rest of his life.

Throughout the Christian East, Saint George is undoubtedly the most popular warrior-saint. In the Coptic churches of Cairo there are now more than twenty relics of the equestrian saint, and in the Orthodox churches in Greece more than one hundred relics of Saint George remind the believer of the victory of the forces of good over evil, the demons, Satan, and the Antichrist. The origins of the Coptic attachment to the chains of Saint George are in the Byzantine traditions. The Convent of Saint George on Büyükada, the largest of the Princes' Islands in the Sea of Marmara southeast of Istanbul, was probably the oldest site using the chains of Saint George for healing. From Constantinople, the medieval center of Eastern Christianity, the cult spread throughout the Mediterranean world. Today, the largest and most popular Saint George sanctuary with his chains is his church in the Muslim village of al-Khadr on the road from Bethlehem to Hebron. In the fifteenth and sixteenth centuries, pilgrims could even see there the prints from the horseshoes of Saint George's white stallion. Since the seventeenth century, the chains of Saint George in the Greek Orthodox Convent of Saint George in Old Cairo have been used to tie up those suffering from nervous disorders, anxiety neuroses, conversion hysterias, obsessional neuroses, and even schizophrenic psychoses. In 1737, Richard Pococke saw the chains: "They say they have the arm of the saint, and they showed me a pillar, to which an iron collar with a chain is fixed, and they say mad people confined in it for three days certainly recover. They informed me that the Turks often try this experiment and having a great admiration for the saint, frequently come and say their prayers here on Friday."

The Coptic Chains of Saint George in Jerusalem

Ever since the beginning of the nineteenth century, the Coptic church in Jerusalem has held some chains of Saint George, now kept in the Monastery of Saint George. These chains were acquired by the archbishop Abra'am (1820–54) to serve the Coptic pilgrims to the Holy Land. Titus Tobler described the healing process in 1850: "Near the church was the cell for the idiots. Here one could see a chain to which the unfortunate person was tied.

In former days, it was believed that when the sick person improved, Saint George would release him without anyone even opening the locks of the chain. The cell has room only for one person." Today the chain is kept in the southwest corner of the sanctuary. I was told that the chain served as a harness for the horse of the saint. The sick place the chain three times around their neck, and their pain disappears.

The Coptic Chains of Saint George in Old Cairo

Large numbers of Copts and Muslims repair on Fridays and Sundays to the Shrine of the Chains of Saint George in the Convent of Saint George in Old Cairo. The 'Coptic chains' have assumed the functions of the medieval chain-cult of the nearby Greek Orthodox Convent of Saint George. There, Greeks from Greece, Lebanon, Cyprus, and Egypt used to assemble for the *panegyris* of Saint George on the night of April 22 to behold the apparition of the celestial rider on his white horse above the dome of the church. Although the Greek population in Egypt has decreased, the Coptic nuns of Saint George have successfully continued the age-old cult. Just as the Greeks claimed the relics of the arm of Saint George, the Coptic nuns also show the bolster with the famous relic of their patron saint. The wonder-working chain, 4.2 meters long, is attached to the south wall of the inner room of the shrine. Normally the chain is applied to women, though I have also seen men seek the blessings of the saint through the chain. Whoever places the halter of the chain around his neck and winds the chain around his body, kissing the chain piously and offering prayers to Saint George, is considered to be in a state of exceptional grace.

I have seen the therapeutic, miraculous chains of Saint George in the Greek Orthodox Monastery of Saint Elias between Jerusalem and Bethlehem; the Greek Orthodox Church of Saint George in Jerusalem; the Chaldean Monastery of Saint George near Ba'wire, Mosul, Iraq; the Monastery of Rabban Hormuzd, northeast of Alqosh, Iraq; the Monastery of Mar Bahnam, southeast of Mosul, Iraq; the Church of Saint George in Tell Isquf, Iraq; the Church of Saint Thomas in Rezaiyeh, Iran; and the Church of Saint Michael in Lemona, Cyprus.

The Footprint of Christ at Sakha

As early as the sixth century, Christians venerated those stones that showed the imprints of some part of the Lord. One of the early examples is the imprint of Christ's arms, hands, and fingers, even his whole face with chin and nose, on the column of the flagellation (at that time still on Mount Zion), as described by the archdeacon Theodosius (530). Antoninus Martyr

(570) saw the very stone in the Praetorium on which Christ stood as he was examined by Pontius Pilate. By 1483, these stones had become as "big as the bottom of a wine cask," according to Felix Fabri, because they had become hollowed out from people rubbing them. In 1280, the Dominican friar Burchard of Mount Sion stood in awe in front of the rock in the Grotto of Gethsemane, which showed the imprints of the head of Christ. In the Armenian Monastery of Saint James in Jerusalem, the pilgrims venerate the imprints of the arm of Christ, which he left on the wall at the time of the hearing before the high priest Annas, the father-in-law of Caiaphas (John 18:13). In the Church of the Ascension on the Mount of Olives, visitors can see the footprints of Jesus Christ as he ascended to heaven. In 1187 the Church of the Ascension was transformed into a mosque. To this day, pilgrims and tourists from east and west venerate this stone and pour oil into the holy imprints of the rock. Another footprint of Jesus is shown in the Basilica di San Sebastiano in the catacombs in Rome. According to tradition, Peter asked Christ, "Quo vadis, Domine?" whereupon the Lord left a footprint on a marble stone, which is exhibited in the Cappella della Reliquie.

In the thirteenth century, Abu al-Makarim reported that there was at the Church of the Holy Virgin at Gabal al-Kaff or Gabal al-Tayr north of Minya the mark of the palm of the hand of the Lord Christ. As the holy family sailed southward, Jesus touched the mountain, "when it bowed in adoration before him. He restored it to its place with his hand, so that the mark of his hand remained impressed on the rock to the present day." Almeric of Jerusalem cut out the piece of the rock with the imprint of the hand of Christ and took it to Syria in 1168.

According to the eighth-century homily by Bishop Zechariah of Sakha, whose relics were unearthed in 1968, the holy family visited Sakha near Kafr al-Shaikh in the Delta. To still the thirst of the wanderers, Jesus put his foot on a rock, under which a source of water was discovered. The imprint of his foot remained on the rock. Later, believers poured oil on this rock and received blessings from it. During the thirteenth century, according to tradition, the rock disappeared from the courtyard of the church. In 1984, while digging in front of the main gate of the church, workmen discovered what is considered to be the lost rock, which is now kept in a glass case inside the church.

The Tree of the Holy Virgin in Matariya

In 2000, on the occasion of the second millennium celebrations of the flight of the holy family to Egypt, the National Egyptian Heritage Revival

Association (NEHRA) agreed to allocate LE5 million for the regeneration of the area around the tree of the Holy Virgin in Matariya. Moreover, because of the interreligious significance of the tree, NEHRA has built a mosque near the site.

The oldest reference to the tree of the Virgin is found in the Arabic Infancy Gospel of the sixth century, based on a Syrian tradition. In the course of their travels the holy family proceeded to a sycamore tree in Matariya. There Jesus dug a well and from it flowed sweet water, and Mary washed the swaddling clothes of her son and dried them on a post. A boy possessed by a devil took one of them down and put it on his head. "Presently the devil came out of his mouth and flew away in the shape of crows and serpents. And the water with the bodily secretion of Jesus led to the growth of balsam."

According to the apocryphal Gospel of Pseudo-Matthew, the Holy Virgin Mary, tired from the travels, found rest in the shade of a palm tree. Jesus, sitting on his mother's lap, bade the palm tree to give his mother of its fruits. The tree bent so low that she could gather as much as she wanted. This tradition is preserved in the nineteenth sura of the Qur'an: "And the pangs of childbirth drove her unto the trunk of the palm tree. She said: 'Oh, would that I had d.ed ere this and had become a thing of naught, forgotten'! Then [one] cried unto her from below her, saying: 'Grieve not! Thy Lord hath placed a rivulet beneath thee, and shake the trunk of the palm tree toward thee, thou wilt cause ripe dates to fall upon thee'" (19:23–25).

An informative early medieval source pertaining to the itinerary of the holy family in Egypt is the homily of Zechariah. The bishop relates how Jesus took Joseph's staff and broke it into little pieces and planted them in the ground. With his hands he dug a well and there flowed from it sweet water which had an exceedingly sweet odor. Jesus watered therewith the pieces of wood which he had planted, and straightaway they took root and put forth leaves and an exceedingly sweet perfume was emitted by them, which was sweeter than any other perfume. And these pieces of wood grew and they called them balsam.

Probably the earliest Western reference to the garden of balsam in 'Babylon on the Nile' is in the *Chronicon,* sometimes called *The History of the Two States,* by the German bishop Otto of Freising (1114–58). A more detailed description of the garden of balsam and the wood of the tree as well as of the spring in which Mary washed the swaddling clothes of her son is found in the report by Burchard of Strasbourg. At the bidding of Frederick I Barbarossa (1120–90), Burchard resided at the court of Saladin. He mentions that the spring was highly venerated by Muslims, who came to the water with candles and incense to practice their religious ablutions. A significant contribution to the method of extraction of the balsam from the tree and the size of the plantation at Matariya is given by the physician and traveler 'Abd al-Latif of Baghdad (1162–1231) in his graphic and detailed *Account of Egypt*. The *Legenda aurea* by Jacobus de Voragine (c. 1263) introduces a new element in the history of the balsam trees. According to him, the balsam trees originated in the gardens of 'Ain Gedi in Judea. Following the exile, Jews brought the trees to Egypt. Others, however, maintain that the trees were introduced to Egypt by Cleopatra. Sometime in the early thirteenth century, relics of balsam trees of Matariya were found in the reliquaries of the churches in Halle and Wittenberg. Apparently pilgrims used to collect twigs from the precious trees. In fact, Burchard of Mount Sion (1280) visited Matariya at the end of the thirteenth century and carried off much balsam wood and bathed in the well in which the Holy Virgin had dipped her son. All pilgrims are unanimous in their observation that the garden of balsam was tilled by Christians only. In a 1336 text, Ludolph of Suchem saw among the Christian guardians four Germans and explained that the balm was obtained either from the fruit of the bush or by boiling the branches. The Muslims recommended its use for nasal troubles, lumbago, or pain in the knee, while the Christians prescribed it for snake bites, toothaches, and poisonings.

In the Middle Ages, the sultan customarily gave to the two Christian patriarchs a portion of the balm. Thus, when De Lannoy (1421) was in Egypt as ambassador of France, the patriarch of the Copts presented him with a vial of pure balm. According to Pero Tafur (c. 1435), only five pilgrims at a time were permitted to enter the garden, and none was allowed to pinch or nip off leaves or twigs to take away with them.

To the Western pilgrims to the Holy Land, Matariya must have seemed like paradise, for the well with its beautiful surroundings was a resort for such wealthy Mamluks as the amir Yashbak, who built a domed house here in which he entertained his master and friend Qaitbey (1467–96). Entrance to the garden cost the pilgrims six ducats, for which sum they could enjoy relaxation and bathing in the pool, the waters of which both Christians and Muslims believed to be holy and medicinal. The Dominican friar Felix Fabri (1483) noticed close to the gate in the garden an immense fig tree. In its hollow trunk, as in a small chapel, two lamps hung, for the tree had once miraculously opened to provide refuge when the holy family was pursued by two brigands. Marino Sanuto (1321) and John Poloner (1421) believed that they had seen the actual palm tree that had bowed to the Holy Virgin so that she might gather dates from it. When the heathens saw this, according to Sanuto, they cut down the palm tree, but it joined itself together again the following night. The marks of the cutting could still be seen at the time of his pilgrimage.

Toward the end of the fifteenth century, the Franciscans had built a simple chapel for occasional services that was also visited by Muslims. The sanctuary enclosed a niche in which Mary used to place her son and that emitted an intense odor of balsam. Moreover, there was a water basin with crystal-clear water to be used for healing various diseases, including leprosy. In the beginning of the seventeenth century, this chapel was converted into a mosque. At first, Christians could enter the building, but after 1660 the entrance was restricted to Muslims. By 1714 the building seems to have collapsed.

Following the death of Qaitbey in 1496 and the subsequent confusion, the balsam trees were weeded out, and the garden with its *saqiya,* or water wheel, was devastated. The knight Arnold von Harff (1497) was an eyewitness to the wanton destruction of the garden.

The new sultan, Salim I (1517–20), decided that balsam trees from the Hijaz region were to be planted in Matariya. However, the experiment lasted only few years. Just nine bushes had somehow survived a strong winter. For the rotten smell of the other bushes, the Muslims held the Jews responsible! Once again in 1575, the Turkish pasha ordered that balsam trees from Mecca be planted, but this attempt also failed. Father Jean Coppin, who served as French consul from 1638 to 1645, had only heard about the balsam trees— they had disappeared.

While the balsam trees disappeared from the reports of the pilgrims, the original sycamore tree of the Virgin gained religious significance. Muslims and Christians visiting the tree would offer candles and incense. In 1656 a portion of the tree had broken away, and the other part followed in 1694 but was rescued by the Franciscans. A sprout of the tree was planted in 1672. This sycamore reached impressive dimensions, as recorded by Gustave Flaubert (1821–80) and Gérard Nerval (1808–55). In 1854, the Egyptologist Heinrich Brugsch visited the garden with the sycamore, which consisted of three large branches and provided wonderful shade, carrying many figs. Numerous graffiti of names and dates in various languages were engraved in the trunk and the branches. In 1906 this tree collapsed as well, and it is only with the aid of several wooden supports that the remains of the tree of the Virgin have survived.

For the festivities of the year 2000 a new tree had been planted, properly watered by a nearby spring issuing out of an artificial cave.

Dreams, Visions, and Apparitions

ലുവ്വ

THE period of the Coptic patriarchates of Cyril VI (1959–71) and Shenuda III (1971–) was marked by several unusual phenomena that were interpreted as signs of divine grace supporting the various efforts of the Coptic renaissance. At no other period in the recorded history of the Coptic Church do we see so many reports of unfamiliar and extraordinary events as during the second part of the twentieth century. It is impossible to present a complete list of all the unusual 'happenings' in the more than seventy Coptic dioceses and hundreds of parishes in Egypt and overseas. A selection of these events must be sufficient.

It is important to remember that most Copts, whether Orthodox, Catholic, or Evangelical, are biblical and traditional fundamentalists, believers who do not question the authenticity of the sources of their Christian faith. Therefore, questions about the 'miraculous' in this purely religious context are utterly irrelevant. Miracles are repeatedly recorded in the Old and New Testaments, in the traditions of the early fathers and ascetics and in the volumes of the *History of the Patriarchs of the Egyptian Church*. Wonders are an indispensible part of the Coptic understanding of their *Heilsgeschichte*. Moreover, miracles are deeply embedded in the understanding of genuine Egyptian religiosity. They are the authentic evidence of God's victory and triumph over Satan and suffering and death.

Instead of raising the question about the 'how' of a particular rare and uncommon event, Copts would tend to inquire about the 'why,' the reason for such an unusual happening. It is only as we are able to shift into this mentality that we 'moderns of the twenty-first century' will begin to appreciate the deep religious atmosphere of the Christians of the Nile. This includes a sympathetic recognition of apparitions of Mary and various angels, blood- and oil-bleeding icons, floating Bibles, and the like. All of these instances have raised sufficient attention among the faithful 'to come, see and believe,' which has always been one of the motivations for pilgrimages. Churches and monasteries and other places that host such events have received through these 'happenings' an additional quality of 'sacredness,' which is enough reason to repair to these sites in anticipation of recapturing something of the original experience.

Dreams and Visions

Dreams and visions are part of the Christian tradition. There are the famous Biblical dreams of the butler and baker of the king of Egypt (Gen. 40:5), or Nebuchadnezzar's dream about the four kingdoms (Dan. 2). God came to Abimelech in a dream by night (Gen. 20:3) and angels to Jacob at Bethel (Gen. 28:12). The Lord spoke with Moses and Aaron and Miriam in a dream (Num. 12:5), and the prophet Isaiah saw the Lord sitting on the throne accompanied by the seraphim (Isa. 6:2). God has always revealed his will in dreams, and there have always been those who could explain and interpret them.

The tradition of the flight of the holy family to Egypt, one of the most popular in the Coptic Church, is a story that has its origins solely in dreams and visions. In his second dream, Joseph, the spouse of the Holy Virgin, was advised by an angel of the Lord to take Mary and the child and flee to Egypt, for Herod was about to search for the child to destroy him (Matt. 2:13). In a third dream, the Lord appeared again to him, saying, "Rise, take the child and his mother, and go to the land of Israel, for those who sought the child's life are dead" (Matt. 2:20). The detailed description of the itinerary of the travels of the holy family, together with Salome the midwife, covering the numerous stopovers in the Delta and the Nile Valley, has been attributed to a vision that the Coptic patriarch Theophilus (384–412) is said to have received from the Holy Virgin. Pope Cyril VI received additional details of the holy family's route in dreams.

Dreams have not only determined the piety of the Copts, but sometimes also the choice of their leadership. Whenever a dispute pertaining to a candidate for the patriarchal see arose among the electors, or they were divided into two or more interest groups, then a supernatural revelation in the form of a dream or a vision would determine the choice of the future patriarch. Demetrius, the twelfth patriarch (d. 230), was chosen because his predecessor Julian (d. 188) had a vision of the angel of God in which the angel told him that Demetrius should be his successor. While still a monk, Benjamin I (623–62) saw in a dream that he would be called to be patriarch. Michael I (743–67) was elected on the basis of a holy man's revelations. And several other patriarchs of the ninth, eleventh, and twelfth centuries were elected successors of Saint Mark on account of dreams in which either the Lord or

Peter appeared to the candidate or to another pious person.

In some churches in the Delta and the Nile Valley, Copts still adhere to the ancient Egyptian practice of therapeutic incubation, a practice that had its origin in the healing dreams in the sanctuaries of Isis, according to Diodorus Siculus (first century B.C.). In pre-Christian Egypt, the sick and demon-possessed repaired to certain temples to spend one or several nights in the sanctuary in hopes of being healed. There, the 'scribe of the house of life,' as the priest was called, would interpret the dreams of the sick and prescribe remedies. This practice continued in the Christian era, and even today, in several Upper Egyptian churches, I have met Copts who have spent a night sleeping on a mat in front of an icon on the altar screen. Especially on the occasion of the annual pilgrimages, Coptic priests attend to the needs of the pilgrims, thereby fulfilling the functions of the former temple scribes. Toward the end of the twentieth century, dreams by certain priests and monks served as a means of ascertaining the identity of the ever-increasing number of relics of anonymous saints that were bestowed upon the parish churches. As early as the fifth century, the archimandrite Shenuda severely criticized the cult of relics of unknown saints. From his censorious words, it appears that even in those days, every church had to have its martyr's shrine enclosing the bones of some nameless dead that had been disinterred and were assumed to be the relics of martyrs. In most cases, the remains were identified as those of martyrs in a dream by some priest or monk.

Like dreams, visions are an integral part of the Christian tradition. A theophanic vision is described at the baptism of Jesus, when those in attendance witnessed the Holy Spirit descend like a dove and alight on Christ (Matt. 3:16). At the transfiguration, Christ, Moses, and Elijah appeared to the apostles Peter, James, and John (Matt. 17:2–9), and at Emmaus the eyes of the two disciples were opened and they recognized Christ, then he vanished out of their sight (Luke 24:31). In their pentecostal vision there appeared to the apostles "tongues as of fire, distributed and resting on each one of them" (Acts 2:3). Paul wrote to the Corinthians that he had seen the Lord, undoubtedly on the road to Damascus (1 Cor. 9:1). In Troas he had a vision of a man of Macedonia beseeching him to come to his country (Acts 16:9), and on his voyage to Rome, after leaving Crete, an angel of God stood by Paul and comforted him (Acts 27:23–24).

Visions of Jesus Christ, the Holy Virgin Mary, the archangels, or certain saints are customary in the Coptic traditions and are often recorded in the biographies of the Coptic saints. The purpose of the vision is to strengthen the recipients' faith and inspire them to pursue the ascetic life or to prepare them for the expected martyrdom. The Coptic synaxarion mentions eleven visions of Jesus Christ, thirty-seven of archangels, and six of the Holy Virgin Mary. Some of the Coptic churches and monasteries were founded on account of visions. Saint John Kame, a contemporary of Pope James (819–30), experienced the presence of the Holy Virgin, who presented him with three solidi (gold coins) to distribute to the destitute at the Monastery of the Syrians in Wadi al-Natrun, which since the ninth century has been dedicated to Saint John Kame. About Pope Matthew I (1378–1408) it is reported that he used to converse repeatedly with the Holy Virgin, who appeared to him in the Church of the Holy Virgin, Harat Zuwayla, Cairo.

In modern times, visions are still very influential in the Coptic Church. A vision of the Holy Virgin decisively determined the spiritual life of young Azer in 1910, who later became Pope Cyril VI, the 116th successor of Saint Mark. Ummina Irene, abbess of the Convent of Saint Mercurius in Old Cairo, used to experience a vision of the Holy Virgin and Saint Mercurius annually on the eve of Easter. Before making any significant decision regarding her convent, she would consult the Holy Virgin and Saint Mercurius. While roaming at night through the Monastery of Saint Antony at the Red Sea, Abuna Yustus al-Antuni (1910–76) repeatedly met Saint Antony either on the wall of the monastery or in the Church of Saint Mark. Ummina Martha (1938–88), abbess of the Convent of Saint Theodore in Harat al-Rum, experienced several visions of the Holy Virgin, Saint Theodore, and Pope Cyril VI. In the spring of 1959, the Holy Virgin ordered her to build a church with three altars. A vision of a special kind is recorded about Abuna Andarawus al-Samwili. Although blind from birth, he saw the Holy Virgin in the form of Carlo Dolci's *Mater Dolorosa* just prior to his death on February 7, 1988. During a visit to the Church of the Resurrection in Jerusalem in 1956, Metropolitan Banyamin saw the Holy Virgin Mary as he celebrated the Divine Liturgy in the Coptic Chapel at the western end of the Tomb of Christ. In the morning hours of November 25, 1987, Mrs. Nahed Muhammad Mitwali, director of the Girls' College in Helmiya al-Zaytun, had a vision of the Holy Virgin as Immaculata. On account of this experience, Mrs. Mitwali accepted the Christian faith and changed her name to Fibe (Phoebe) Salib. Her change of religion led to several severe threats from Muslims.

Apparitions

At one time, such private visions and apparitions were extremely rare. Today, however, we are flooded with reports of them. It is almost impossible to know how many of them are authentic and how many are the result of the influence of the news media, which focuses on the sensational. In all of these cases it is the responsibility of the episcopal committee to investigate well-founded reports of allegedly miraculous events that have occurred in the dioceses. Because of the increasing number of reports of visions and apparitions of the Holy Virgin, angels, and saints, it is imperative to agree upon certain procedures and standards. At the end of the investigative process, the diocesan committee of the Holy Synod makes one of three conclusions: the event shows all the signs of being an authentic or a truly miraculous intervention (*constat de supernaturalitate*); the alleged apparition is clearly not miraculous or there are not sufficient signs manifesting it to be so (*constat de non supernaturalitate*); or it is not clear whether or not the alleged apparition is authentic (*non constat de supernaturalitate*).

Furthermore, it is difficult to differentiate between 'endogenous' visions, or private revelations, namely those having originated through a purely individual 'awareness,' and those more spectacular 'exogenous' apparitions, which are said to have been produced through external causes. Also, in the latter case, the receptivity of the individual and the group is a decisive factor. These apparitions involving small or large groups unwittingly create a kind of 'snowball' effect that inspires pilgrimages to such 'blessed sites,' be they churches or monasteries.

In a documentary entitled *Apparitions and Messages of the Mother of God of the Past Two Thousand Years,* G. Hierzenberger and O. Nedomansky (Augsburg, 1998) have listed more than nine hundred apparitions. The International Marian Research Institute in Dayton, Ohio, accepted by the Roman Catholic Church (1998), has registered in the twentieth century alone 386 mariophanies, or apparitions of Mary.

Apparitions ought to be seen as revelations of the will and purpose of God in time and space. Many of them have been recorded in the traditions of the Christian churches in the East and in the West. The most important twentieth-century apparition of the Holy Virgin without the Christ child in Egypt occurred on the night of April 2, 1968, on the dome of the Church of the Holy Virgin at Shari' Tumanbey in the Cairene suburb of Zaytun, near Matariya, where almost two thousand years before she had rested with the Christ child, Joseph, and Salome. Although the Holy Virgin did not deliver a message, as she did at Lourdes (1858) and Fatima (1917), Copts have interpreted the visit of the Holy Virgin as God's response to Egyptians' desperate economic and political situation after their disastrous defeat by the Israelis in the 1967 War, and moreover they regarded the apparition as a way of blessing Copts, who were not able to visit the Christian holy places in Nazareth, Bethlehem, and Jerusalem.

In September 1982, about a year after Pope Shenuda III had been exiled by President Anwar al-Sadat to the Monastery of Bishoi in Wadi al-Natrun, the Holy Virgin appeared in the Church of the Holy Virgin in Shari'a al-Gumhuriya in the Upper Egyptian town of Idfu. The apparition was taken as a sign of comfort and hope for the Copts, who were without their shepherd.

During the Lenten season of 1986, the Holy Virgin appeared on March 25 on the roof between the two belfries of the Church of Saint Damiana on Shari'a Muhammad 'Abd al-Muta'il, Ard Baba Dublu, Shubra, Cairo. These apparitions happened outside and inside of the church. In April 1986 Pope Shenuda III appointed a papal committee consisting of four bishops, two priests, and a layman to pass an opinion on the matter. Whereas the Zaytun apparition of 1968 was entered as a feast of the Holy Virgin under the date of April 2 in the official calendar of commemorations, the same privilege was not extended to the other apparitions. Most recently, on the occasion of the pilgrimage on August 22, 1990, several apparitions of the Holy Virgin were reported from the pilgrimage center at Dair Durunka south of Asyut.

In 1995 and 1996, Copts and Muslims from Cairo and the province of Sharqiya repaired to the village of Kafr Yusuf Samri south of al-Zaqaziq to behold the apparition of the archangel Michael in the Church of Saint Michael, who appeared both dressed in a white *galabiya* and as a bright shining light. Pilgrims reported various miracles on account of the apparition, including the multiplication of oil and many healings.

During the days prior to the feast of the Assumption on August 22, 1997, the Holy Virgin appeared repeatedly on the roof and in the Church of the Holy Virgin in the village of Shantana al-Hagar in Minufiya. Pope Shenuda III sent a committee of five bishops to investigate the claims. They confirmed the apparitions and reported to have seen the Holy Virgin greeting and blessing the pilgrims, more than 150,000 of whom are said to have visited the small village between Quwaisna and Tanta. Unfortunately, some Muslim fanatics disrupted the pilgrimages to Shantana al-Hagar. Even weeks later, visitors to the church were searched by the local police. In March 1999, the Holy Virgin appeared again in the Church of Saint Menas in Minya al-Qamh, Sharqiya. Because of the many witnesses to this apparition, Pope Shenuda III delegated a committee of three bishops to investigate. After lengthy discussions with the local bishop and members of the parish the delegation reached the decision *constat non supernaturalitate!* Was their decision due to concern about possible violent reactions by Islamic extremists, as had happened in Shantana al-Hagar? To protect interreligious peace, the local bishop prohibited any form of pilgrimage to the Church of Saint Menas in Minya al-Qamh.

When I visited the Church of Saint George in the village of Birma, northwest of Tanta, Gharbiya, in April 2000, the parishioners told me that on New Year's Day 2000 the Holy Virgin appeared in their church. Signs on one of the columns testify to the apparition. On Thursday and Friday, August 17 and 18, 2000, large numbers of Christians of different churches and Muslims witnessed the apparition of the Holy Virgin Mary between the belfries and above the domes of Saint Mark's Church on Shari' Mutraniya in Asyut. The apparition continued each day for several hours and was accompanied by flocks of birds. Metropolitan Michael of Asyut has appointed a committee to investigate these phenomena.

It is noteworthy that all mariophanies in Egypt between 1968 and 2000 have appeared as the Immaculata of the Miraculous Medallion, the image of the Virgin with arms outspread that was seen in 1830 by Cathérine Labouré of the Convent of the Daughters of Charity. This image of the Holy Virgin seems to have impressed itself so much on the religious consciousness of the Copts that it has dislodged all traditional Coptic images of the Holy Virgin that were created by eighteenth- and nineteenth-century iconographers.

Coptic Saints in an Age of Globalization

THE theology and piety of any group, Copts or otherwise, is always a reflection of its cultural, social, and economic climate. During the past five decades, rural and industrial developments have radically altered the lives of millions of Egyptians. Old lifestyles and patterns have given way to new modes of living. The churches, rather than being prophetic spearheads of these dramatic social changes, seemed to be engaged in rearguard actions. For the first time in its long history, the leadership of the Coptic Church must direct its spiritual message and charitable efforts at four social groups of believers, which—on various levels—are in constant interaction. These are the tradition-oriented farmers (*fellahin*) of Lower and Upper Egypt, a rapidly growing industrially employed urban population that is continually exposed and challenged with secularist values, an educated middle and upper class of the towns and cities, and an ever-increasing number of emigrants, either periodically to the Gulf states or permanently to the Western world.

The tradition-oriented farmers have been mercilessly catapulted from a more or less enclosed village society into a modern world of international displays and experiences. As Bishop Thomas of al-Qusiya and Meir describes it:

> Once, the villages of Upper Egypt were virtually cut off from the rest of the world, but today I estimate that more than sixty percent of the villagers in my diocese have at least one satellite dish. The households possessing a dish want to show their possessions off to others, and soon it becomes a business to have others watch it. Information is shared, topics are discussed, habits and customs influenced. Many more homes possess the simple tape recorder, so that the influence of modern music on traditional church and folk music is great.

Nonetheless, the farmers' attachment to the saints is still very real. They depend on the intercession of their patrons not only for a productive harvest but also for the health and well-being of their families. The statistics of the

Upper Egyptian pilgrimage centers reveal a remarkable increase in pilgrims to the annual festivities of the Holy Virgin Mary in June and August. At the same time, not all Coptic bishops support the pilgrimages of their peoples and question the religious values of the *mawalid.*

The industrially employed urban population constitutes a challenge to all churches. Many families have moved from the country to the cities in expectation of better working and living conditions. Often they are settled in the new satellite suburbs, where they are socially and religiously disconnected. They are confronted with the material wealth, prosperity, and fortune that the city offers. Their religious needs are real, but the bustle and speed of city life often prevents them from taking time for the necessary spiritual 'refueling.' Tens of thousands of these Christians, the majority of them young men and women, attend every Wednesday evening the meetings, sermons, and spiritual lectures by Pope Shenuda III at the Cathedral of Saint Mark in 'Abbasiya. Many of them serve in the parochial Sunday schools. To them the lives of the Coptic saints are a spiritual reality. They carry the devotional pictures of their patron saints, along with a bit of the *hanut,* the sacred spice mixture, in their wallets, pocketbooks, or handbags. Many of them have seen the mariophanies of Zaytun, Ard Baba Dublu, Shantana al-Hagar, Minya al-Qamh, or Asyut and felt enriched and blessed by these spiritual events. The Copts of the urban middle class are exposed to the secular values that determine their social and economic life. Those with a traditional family background continue in observing the major Christian fasts and feasts; others have largely followed the modern "Zeitgeist," that is not areligious, but indifferent to the teachings and practices of the church.

The attentive observer of the religious scene in Egypt may notice that since the mariophanies of Zaytun in 1968, there has been a multiplicity of recordings of apparitions of angels and the Holy Virgin Mary. These are said to have occurred in the sanctuaries and on the domes of the churches in the villages and towns of Lower and Upper Egypt. In fact, one gains the impression that in a world of rapid competitive social and economic developments, there is a need, a necessity even, for 'religious novelties.' The inroads of the various electronic devices, of computers and modern means of mass communication, have menaced or even threatened a largely tradition-oriented, conservative group of believers. Therefore, the reliance upon celestial comfort in the form of heavenly apparitions and light appearances and the like seem understandable and should be seen as a kind of 'religious defense mechanism' against a new world with its electronic threats. The same quest for 'novelty' has also led to new discoveries of relics of saints, through either excavations or dreams.

As a minority the Copts are in many ways unique. During certain periods in the early Middle Ages, all Egyptian Christians were compelled by the Islamic authorities to identify themselves as believers in Jesus Christ. They were obliged to wear heavy wooden crosses around their necks. Today, the Copts carry simpler labels to assure their identity. In Egypt more than in any other Middle Eastern country, the name of a person betrays his religious and ethnic identity. Coptic names are inclusive, drawing on pharaonic roots as well as a number of other languages. Following the introduction of Christianity in the Nile Valley, Egyptians who had accepted the Christian faith selected names of Biblical personages, church fathers, saints, monks, and hermits. Thus many Hebrew-Aramaic, Greek, and Latin names were introduced into Egypt. At the same time, many pre-Christian names were preserved because their bearers, who were martyrs, saints, or monks, had been canonized. This is especially true of many pharaonic names, such as Amon, Hor, and Sarapamon. During the Hellenistic, Roman, and Byzantine eras, Copts adopted Greek and Latin names. After the Arab conquest, Coptic and Greek names were often translated into Arabic: for example, Christodoulus became 'Abd al-Masih. During the French occupation and more so during British rule, numerous Copts gave their children Western names like Cromer, Kitchener, Henry, and William. Although in Egypt there is a trend toward religiously neutral names, names that could by used by Christians and Muslims, in the emigration Copts largely follow the name-giving customs of their new environment.

The Coptic language provides a less concrete sense of identity; its use has been an issue ever since the early Middle Ages. As early as the twelfth century, Pope Gabriel II (1131–45) admonished the priests to explain the Lord's Prayer in the vernacular Arabic. In the thirteenth and fourteenth centuries, Coptic liturgical books begin to have an Arabic translation side by side with the Coptic text. In Upper Egypt, Coptic seems to have prevailed much longer. Al-Maqrizi implies that Coptic was still spoken in the monasteries around Asyut in the fifteenth century. It is generally believed that Coptic ceased to be a spoken language in the seventeenth century, and is now purely a liturgical language.

Ethnically, the Copts consider themselves the true Egyptians, sons and daughters of the pharaohs. Just as the Assyrian Christians in Mesopotamia consider themselves heirs of Hammurabi and Assurbanipal, and the Lebanese Maronites believe that they are the successors of Hiram and Ithobal, so the Copts point with pride to their ancestry beginning with Menes, the founder of the First Dynasty in 2900 B.C. Whereas from a Biblical point of view the Copts, the Mizraim, were the grandchildren of Noah through Ham (Gen.

10:6), ethnically speaking they are North Africans. Their use of the Arabic language identifies them with the pan-Arab world extending from the Atlantic Ocean to the Persian Gulf. As Arabic-speaking Christians, the Copts share their faith in Jesus Christ with the other arabophone Christians of the Middle East, be they Orthodox, Catholic, or Protestant.

Theologically the Copts are Biblical fundamentalists adhering to the doctrine of the verbal infallibility of the Holy Scriptures. They accept the teachings of the first three ecumenical councils, Nicea (325), Constantinople (381), and Ephesus (431), and those of the pre-Chalcedonian fathers, Saints Justin, Irenaeus, Clement of Alexandria, Hippolytus, Ephraem Syrus, Cyprian, and the three Cappadocian fathers. They also accept the teachings of the Egyptian and Syrian post-Chalcedonian fathers, such as Severus of Antioch, James of Sarug, and the pontifical Alexandrian-Antiochene synodicons of the ninth to the eleventh century. The Copts also hold to the canons of the seven fourth- and fifth-century synods of Ancyra, Neocaesarea, Gangra, Antioch, Laodicea, Sardica and Carthage. For their liturgical and disciplinary life, they follow the thirty-one canons of Christodoulus, the forty-three canons of Cyril II, the thirty-two canons of Gabriel II, and the canon law by Cyril III.

The Coptic Church has responded to the fact that hundreds of thousands of the faithful have left the banks of the Nile. Hundreds of churches have been established in the Western world with the intent to provide a spiritual home for emigrants. The Coptic Church has clearly decided to preserve at least its theological identity in the emigration, even if the ethnic identity may somehow evaporate over the years. To retain a Coptic theological identity requires an unusually competent, well-trained, and highly motivated clergy. It is hoped that the Coptic Church, facing the global responsibilities of the twenty-first century, will be in a position to muster the required priests, youth workers, administrators, and bishops for this task.

Bibliography of the Author's Studies in Periodicals

❧❧❧

Abbreviations of Periodicals

BSAC	*Bulletin de la Société d'Archéologie Copte,* Cairo
CCR	*Coptic Church Review,* Lebanon, Penn., USA
COP	*Coptologia,* Don Mills, Ontario, Canada
DCO	*Der Christliche Osten,* Würzburg, Germany
FMeth	*Festschrift Methodios,* London, 1985
HERM	*Hermeneia, Ztschr. f. Ostkirchliche Kunst,* Bochum, Germany
IFAO	Institut Français d'Archéologie Orientale du Caire, Cairo
IKZ	*Internationale Kirchliche Zeitschrift,* Bern, Switzerland
KMT	*Kemet, Ztschr. f. Ägyptenfreunde,* Berlin, Germany
MMES	*Medieval and Middle Eastern Studies,* Leiden, 1972
OkSt	*Ostkirchliche Studien,* Würzburg, Germany
OrChr	*Oriens Christianus,* Wiesbaden, Germany
OrSu	*Orientalia Suecana,* Uppsala, Sweden
SOC	*Studia Orientalia Christiana Collectanea,* Cairo

Biblical Saints in Coptic Spirituality

1. The Holy Virgin Mary

"The Episkepsis of Dair al-Abiad," *SOC* 15 (1973): 99–106.

"Recent Developments in Coptic Mariology," *CCR* 13, no. 3 (1992): 82–90; *SOC* 24 (1991): 371–80.

"Carol Dolci's Mater Dolorosa in Coptic Piety," *OrSu* 41 (1992): 155–65.

"Von der 'Immaculata' zur 'Mater Dolorosa,'" *KMT* 3, no. 2 (1994): 25–27.

"Die Ohrenempfängnis Mariens bei den Kopten," *KMT* 8, no. 1 (1999): 40–41.

"Kopt. Chronologie und Ikonographie Mariens," *DCO* 55, no. 5 (2000): 225–33, *KMT* 10, 3, 2001.

2. Joseph, Spouse of the Holy Virgin
"Coptic Chronology and Iconography of Saint Joseph," *COP* 18 (forthcoming).
"Zur Koptischen Chronologie und Ikonographie des hl. Joseph," *KMT* 11, 1, 2002.
3. The Old Testament Patriarchs and Prophets
"The Relics of Saint John the Baptist and the Prophet Elisha" *OkSt* 29 (1980): 118–42.
4. The Holy Apostles
"Die Altarschranken im Dair Anba Bishoi," *OkSt* 36, no. 3 (1937): 178–85.
"The Four Evangelists in Popular Art," *SOC* 16 (1981): 191–97.
5. The Heavenly Host and the Twenty-four Elders of the Apocalypse
"The 24 Elders in the Iconography of the Copts," *SOC* 13 (1968): 141–58.
"Die himmlischen Heerscharen bei den Kopten," *KMT* 7, no. 2 (1998): 42–44.
"The Heavenly Host in Coptic Tradition," *CCR* 21, no. 2 (2000): 137–40.

The Martyrs in Coptic Spirituality
"The Martyrdom of Sidhom Bishai," *COP* 11 (1990): 65–71; *DCO* 46, no. 6 (1991): 333–35.
"Die Heiligen der Mameluckenzeit," *KMT* 9, no. 1 (2000): 43–47.

The Ascetics in Coptic Spirituality
"Recent Developments in Monasticism," *OrChr* 49 (1965): 79–89.
"The Hermits of Wadi Rayan," *SOC* 11 (1966): 273–318.
"Monastische Erneuerungen," *OrChr* 61 (1977): 59, 70.
"Die Kaiserssöhne in der Wüste," *OrChr* 70 (1986): 181–87.
"Zur monastischen Erneuerung," *DCO* 41 (1986): 210–17.
"Zeitgenössische Gottesnarren in Ägypten," *OkSt* 36, no. 4 (1987): 301–10.
"Revival of Upper Egyptian Monasticism," *COP* 8 (1987): 67–74.
"Zum Hl. Barsum dem Nackten," *DCO* 46, no. 8 (1991): 336–39.
"Saint Antonius und Qimn al-Arus," *KMT* 4, no. 2 (1995): 41–42.
"Saint John Colobus–Kloster," *KMT* 6, no. 3 (1997): 43–45.
"Zu Ehren der Altäre erhoben," *DCO* 53, no. 2 (1998): 108–18; *CCR* 19, no. 3 (1998): 83–90.
"Multikulturelle Wüstenökumene" *KMT* 7, no. 4 (1998): 40–44.
"Saint Bishoi als Christophorus," *HERM* 15, no. 1 (1999): 12–15.
"Einsiedler Ägyptens Einst und Heute," *KMT* 9, no. 1 (2000): 47–51.

The Equestrian Warriors in Coptic Spirituality
"The Martyria of Saints," *MMES* (1972): 311–43.
"Saint Mercurius-Abu al-Saifain," *SOC* 15 (1973): 109–20.
"The Equestrian Deliverer" *OrChr* 57 (1973): 142–55.
"Zeitgenössische Volksfrömmigkeit," *OrSu* 40 (1991): 164–80.

The 'Silverless' Physicians in Coptic Spirituality
"A Coptic Anargyros: Saint Colluthus," *SOC* 14 (1971): 365–75.
"Apa Klog of al-Fant," *COP* 7 (1986): 39–43.
"Silberlose Ärzte," *KMT* 8, no. 2 (1999): 48–50.

The Women Saints in Coptic Spirituality
"The Cult of Saint Damiana" *OrSu* 18 (1970): 45–68.
"Saint Barbara in the Coptic Cult," *SOC* 15 (1973): 121–32.
"Sitt Rifqah and Her Five Children," *FMeth* (1985): 457–77.
"Renaissance der koptischen Nonnenklöster" *OkSt* 37, no. 1 (1988): 23–30;
    KMT 3, no. 2 (1994): 27–29.
"Koptische Frauen für die Ewigkeit geweiht," *KMT* 8, no. 4 (1999): 34–38.

Recently Discovered Martyrs
"Die Mumien von Naqlun," *OrChr* 80 (1996): 98–107; *CCR* 15, no. 3
    (1994): 73–80; *KMT* 7, no. 1 (1998): 48–50.
"The Rediscovery of Coptic Saints," *CCR* 19, no. 3 (1998): 83–90; *DCO* 53,
    no. 2 (1998): 109–18.

The Veneration of Saints
"An Inventory of Coptic Relics," *OkSt* 17 (1968): 134–73.
"1000 Jahre Koptischer Reliquienkult," *DCO* 51, no. 2 (1996): 113–22.
"Die Renaissance und ihre Wunder," *DCO* 51, no. 5 (1996): 261–5.
"The Mystery of the Akhmim Martyrs" *CCR* 21, no. 4 (2000): 132-138;
    KMT 11, no 2 (2002).

The Coptic Pilgrimage
"The Itinerary of the Holy Family," *SOC* 7 (1962): 2–48.
"Coptic Pilgrimage Testimonies," *OrSu* 24 (1975): 3–6.
"Bir al-Ain bei Achmim," *OkSt* 34, no. 3 (1985): 183–86.
"Dair al-Muharraq: Jerusalem der Kopten," *KMT* 2, no. 4 (1993): 21–23.
"Alt-Kairo: Saints Sergius and Bacchus," *KMT* 5, no. 3 (1996): 31–40.
"Alt-Kairo: Saint Barbara," *KMT* 5, no. 4 (1996): 44–45.
"Der koptische Mulid," *KMT* 6, no. 1 (1997): 47–48.

"Biblische Erfüllungserzählung: Die heilige Familie," *KMT* 6, no. 4 (1997): 36–43.

"Fajumklöster einst und jetzt," *KMT* 7, no. 1 (1998): 46–48.

"Die Kettenheilungen des Saint Georg," *KMT* 9, no. 4 (2000): 47–49.

Dreams, Visions, and Apparitions

"Mystical Phenomena among the Copts," *OkSt* 15, no. 4 (1966): 143–53, 289–307.

"The Apparition of the Holy Virgin in 1986," *OkSt* 35, no. 4 (1986): 337–39.

"Die Renaissance und ihre Wunder," *DCO* 51, no. 5 (1996): 261–65.

"Die Marienerscheinungen einst und heute," *KMT* 8, no. 4 (1999): 39–43.

Coptic Saints in an Age of Globalization

"Theological Issues of the Coptic Orthodox Inculturation in Western Society," *CCR* 18, no. 3 (1997): 67–77.

Index